THE TOWER OF BABBLING

A Self-Study Guide and Career Considerations for
Independent Learners of Any Foreign Language

by Keith Hayden
edited by Ajani Abdul-Khaliq

Social Arts
2019

The Tower of Babbling

Copyright © 2019 by Keith Hayden

All rights reserved. This book or any portion thereof may not be reproduced or used in any manner whatsoever without the express written permission of the publisher except for the use of brief quotations in a book review or scholarly journal.

First Printing: 2019

ISBN: 978-1-7337455-1-2

Social Arts & Technical Alliance
7979 Broadway #209
San Antonio, TX 78209

https://thesata.com

Ordering Information:
Special discounts are available on quantity purchases by corporations, associations, educators, and others. For details, contact the publisher at the above listed address.

Contents

Methods sections are in blue

Introduction 1
   Why I Wrote This Book.. 1
   What This Book Is... 8
   What This Book Isn't.. 9
   Language Fluency vs. Language Literacy 10

Getting Started (Chapter 1) 13
   How to Use This Book (Students) 13
      Step 1: Determine Your Current Language Level........ 14
      Step 2: Go to the Applicable Level 22
      Step 3: Gather the Materials.................................... 24
      Step 4: Design Your Study Plan............................... 24
      Step 5: Track Your Progress..................................... 25
   How to Use This Book (For Language Teachers) 27
      Using the Language Journal...................................... 28
      Designing Assignments (In And Out Of Class) 28
      Helping With Self-Assessments 28
      A Self-Study Mindset 29
   A Note for Heritage Language Learners 30
   A Final Note for Experienced Language Learners............ 31

Beginner Level (Chapter 2) 33
   Who Is A Beginner Learner?.. 33
   Action Items for Beginners 34
      Find One or Two Tools... 34

- Research the Language 34
- Have Fun With It! 35
- Things to Avoid: Beginners 35
- Sample Study Plan for Beginners 37
- Estimated Length Of Time At The Beginner Level? 38
- How to Know When to Move On To the Next Level 38
- General Notes on the Beginner Level 38
  - How to Avoid Giving Up 39
- Beginner Level Quick Notes 40

Advanced Beginner Level (Chapter 3) 41
- Who Is An Advanced Beginner? 41
- Action Items for Advanced Beginners 42
  - A bilingual dictionary 42
  - A reliable grammar resource 42
  - Phonetics 42
  - Deliberate writing 43
  - Short and easy dialogues 44
  - Considering tutors 45
- Things to Avoid: Advanced Beginners 48
- Sample Study Plans for Advanced Beginners 52
- Estimated Length Of Time At The Advanced Beginner Level? 53
- How to Know When to Move On To the Next Level 54
- General Notes on the Advanced Beginner Level 55
- Advanced Beginner Level Quick Notes 55

Contents

Intermediate Level (Chapter 4) 57
    Who Is An Intermediate Learner? 58
    Action Items for Intermediate Learners: Vocabulary 58
        Building your vocabulary 58
    Things to Avoid: Intermediate Vocabulary 71
    Action Items for Intermediate Learners: Studying Grammar 72
        Solidifying Your Grammar 72
        On Verb Conjugation 73
    Things to Avoid: Intermediate Grammar 75
    Action Items for Intermediate Learners: Intermediate Reading 76
    Things to Avoid: Intermediate Reading 77
    Action Items for Intermediate Learners: Intermediate Speaking 78
        Conversation Partners 78
    Things to Avoid: Intermediate Speaking 80
    Action Items for Intermediate Learners: Intermediate Listening 80
        Native speaker content 81
        Watching easy materials 81
        Realistic dialogues 82
    Things to Avoid: Intermediate Listening 84
    Action Items for Intermediate Learners: Intermediate Writing 87
        Texting 88
        Taking notes 88

- Journalling 89
- Things to Avoid: Intermediate Writing 91
- Sample Study Plan for Intermediate Learners 92
  - Cautions 93
- Estimated Length Of Time At The Intermediate Level? ... 95
- How to Know When to Move On To the Next Level 96
- General Notes on the Intermediate Level 98
- On the Plateau 99
  - Getting off of the plateau 100
  - Final thoughts on the plateau 103
- Intermediate Level Quick Notes 104

Advanced Level (Chapter 5) 109
- Who is an Advanced Learner? 110
  - A Word of Congratulations 110
- Action Items for Advanced Learners: Advanced Vocabulary 111
  - Continue Building Your Vocabulary! 111
- Things to Avoid: Advanced Vocabulary 113
- Action Items for Advanced Learners: Advanced Reading 113
  - Reading the news 114
  - Reading books 114
- Things to Avoid: Advanced Reading 120
- Action Items for Advanced Learners: Advanced Speaking 123
  - Taking it on the road 123
- Things to Avoid: Advanced Speaking 131

Contents

So what's the best way to learn idioms?.................... 134
Action Items for Advanced Learners: Advanced Listening
.... 135
    No more teaching materials 135
    Movies in the target language........................ 136
    Repeating unfamiliar words 136
    Words by native speakers. 136
    Focusing on cultural context 137
    Watch the more than once............................. 137
    Suggested progression of materials 137
    The Pros and Cons of Music......................... 139
Things to Avoid: Advanced Listening 142
Action Items for Advanced Learners: Advanced Writing
.... 143
    Group forums 144
    Blogs.. 144
    Practicing for a writing test 145
Things to Avoid: Advanced Writing..................... 146
Studying Culture.. 147
Sample Study Plans for Advanced Learners 152
Things to Avoid: Advanced Study Schedule.................. 153
Estimated Length Of Time At the Advanced Level?...... 153
How to Know When to Move On To the Next Level? .. 154
    Testing your Speaking 155
    Testing your Listening.................................... 156
    Testing your Reading 157

Testing your Writing 157
General Notes about the Advanced Level 159
Advanced Level Quick Notes 160

Native-Like Level (Chapter 6) 165
Being a Native-Like Speaker 166
Who Is A Person At The Native-Like Level? 166
Action Items for Native-Like Speakers 167
    Specialize 167
    Entertain yourself 167
    Master storyteller 168
General Notes on This Level 174
Native-Like Level Quick Notes 182

The Professional Language Learner's Toolkit (Chapter 7)
.. 185
From Hobbyist to Professional 185
Types of Language Jobs 186
Language Credentialing 188
Standing Out As a Language Professional 189
    Language Degrees 189
    Online Language Courses 190
    Formal Tests 191
    Formal Language Immersion Programs 192
    Informal Language Immersion 194
    Non-Class Language Resources as Experience 195

The Future of Foreign Languages (Chapter 8) 199
New Hope 203

Contents

Strengthening Communities 203
Conclusion 204

Appendix 1, Resources 207

Appendix 2, Formal Tests 209

American Council on the Teaching of Foreign Languages (ACFTL) Oral Proficiency Interview (OPI) Tests 209
American Sign Language 211
Arabic 211
Bahasa Indonesian 211
Bahasa Melayu 211
European Consortium for the Certificate of Attainment in Modern Languages (ECL) 211
Burmese 212
Chinese - Mandarin 212
Czech 213
Danish 213
Dutch 213
English 213
Estonian 215
Finnish 215
French 215
Galician 215
German 216
Greek 216
Irish 216
Italian 216
Japanese 216

Tower of Babbling

Kazakh	217
Klingon	217
Korean	217
Latvian	217
Lithuanian	217
Norwegian	217
Polish	218
Portuguese (Brazilian)	218
Portuguese (European)	218
Russian	218
Serbo-Croatian	218
Slovak	219
Spanish	219
Swedish	219
Thai	219
Turkish	219
Vietnamese	220
Welsh	220

Introduction

Why I Wrote This Book

"Focus on conveying meaning, not individual words." This is advice that I read time and time again throughout my studies to become a language interpreter, and I often think about it when I communicate in a language other than my mother tongue. In its basic form, a language is a collection of sounds and utterances expressed in a certain way that convey meaning. Each language contains its own code for organizing those elements, but if you can crack the code you can easily add other elements to it (words, intonation, etc.) to make the language mean something. Despite the relative simplicity of what a language is, the task of going from a person interested in the language, to being able to communicate in it smoothly and coherently is monumental. When we think about the years and decades that it took for us to acquire the modest language ability that we possess in our native language (or languages), the thought of having that capability and capacity of expression in another language seems that much more impossible to imagine. But the reality is that people do it, and it usually doesn't take them decades to do so. How do they do it? Luckily for you, for the past decade I have spent a large amount of time trying to figure out how to learn foreign languages more efficiently. This book is the result of those experiences and efforts.

I love foreign languages. I took two years of French in high school and obtained a minor in Japanese in college. After improving my Japanese through self-study, I was privileged to live and work in Okinawa, Japan, for a period of two years through the military. After being in Japan, I moved to Hawaii, where I had the opportunity to pick up some basic Korean, travel to Korea, speak more Japanese, return to Japan a few times, and begin to learn Spanish as well.

I mention all of this to say that, I'm no stranger to learning foreign languages whether it's in a formal academic environment or on my own. They are a window into the true nature of foreign cultures and have broadened my mind and life profoundly. Which is why I in 2016, I decided to dedicate myself to learning Spanish full-time in order to be able to use it as a language interpreter. I didn't want to just be fluent, I wanted to have an almost native understanding of the language, which included being able to write and read in the language in formal and informal environments.

It was a lofty goal that I jumped into with enthusiasm; however, even with all of my experience learning languages up to that point in my life, and a burning desire and necessity to learn Spanish, I still struggled.

I used nearly every tool imaginable: hard copy books, e-books, webinars, online courses, the latest apps, YouTube videos, private tutors (online and offline), volunteering, I even traveled to Nicaragua to practice my Spanish in a

Introduction

foreign environment. While all of these things did help me progress, the moments when I found them were almost random, and like the pieces of a puzzle, didn't seem to come together at the right times for my overall language development.

Finding these language learning materials was the easy part. It was knowing at what phases of my language training and how to implement them to the maximum benefit that I struggled with.

After nearly two years of trial and error, and thousands of dollars and hours spent, I managed to achieve my goal with Spanish after finally perfecting my study method. Upon reflecting on my language journey, I couldn't help but think that I could have reached my goal sooner if I had been able to solidify a more reliable and more structured method to learn sooner. I wrote this book to address this issue as well.

I personally haven't met any person who became fluent, much less literate, in a foreign language after taking academic classes. The ones who did manage to learn it early on in life when they were of school age and taking those classes, probably spoke it regularly at home with parents and family members, but that fact is of no use for an adult who desires to reach a high level in another language.

The fact is, most people that I've met who are proficient in another language either had formal training (non-academic) through an organization like the government, military, or an institution of higher learning or they were self-taught. Since most people have no desire to join some type of federal service, or pay a large sum of money for an effective, yet costly organized language program, this book will serve anyone who wishes to learn **any** foreign language on their own time.

One of the greatest advantages of living in the information age is that it is very easy for anyone to teach themselves almost anything, at any time. The dark side of this however, is that it can be hard to structure your learning. A lack of structure can quickly lead to a lack of focus, which can result in wasted time and money, two things that most of us have in limited supply.

Much of the information in this book has originated from my experiences of trying to create structure in my own learning after over a decade of teaching myself various foreign languages. During that time, I have used countless language tools, yet I have never seen a practical guide that was designed help take someone from a person interested in learning a language, all the way to language literacy and fluency. My goal in writing this book is to provide you with that very resource.

There are thousands of courses, books, materials, apps, websites etc. to learn foreign languages, and that number increases with each passing day. The majority are targeted at beginners or people who are "language interested" (the largest market of learners), and market themselves as the only tool that students need to become fluent. Most fail to deliver the fluency that they promise, and worse yet, they don't provide students with a method to structure their own self-study in order to continue on with their training after they have completed all of the available material within that resource. I do not claim that this book will be your

Introduction

golden key to unlocking your language skills. In fact, I will tell you now in this introduction, that this book is meant to be used **in conjunction with** tools that you have chosen for your target language. This book is as language-neutral as possible, but does contain a few examples of Spanish and Japanese, as those are the two languages other than English that I am most comfortable and familiar with.

Furthermore, I wrote this book because the majority of books today tend to focus on the latest technology (apps, programs, methods etc.) that are available to learn a language. These books may prove useful while a new piece of technology is in fashion; however, in the 21st century, technology changes at such a rapid pace that it seems like most books that focus on specific resources related to technology are outdated by the time, or shortly after, they are published. I believe this trend will continue to be an issue from this point forward; therefore, my intention with this book is to make the **process** of learning a foreign language take center stage, instead of technology. I do mention some tools for anecdotal purposes and provide a small resource section of tools that have been particularly useful for me for completeness. But if you are reading this at some point in the distant future, don't be surprised if most or all of them are obsolete or even out of use by that time. Though don't despair, the blueprint for learning a language presented in this book is designed to endure the test of time and even be used in the complete absence of modern technology. Although admittedly, it would be much more difficult and time consuming to learn a language without internet access, as long as you have someone to teach you and/or a reliable written resource, and a desire to learn, you can learn any foreign language.

Another problem that students of languages face in the 21st century is an overwhelming amount of information.

It can be difficult to find resources that are appropriate for your unique goals among the countless books, videos, online/offline courses, apps, blogs etc. that claim to be able to help students reach their language goals. There are so many options that a student can quickly get overwhelmed by them all and fail to advance or worse, give up all together. This book will help you sort through the available resources for your target language and help you choose the **right tools** for the **right moments** of your language training. This will make your self-study as efficient and effective as possible for meeting your personal goals with the language.

We live in the digital information age, and as such, this book assumes that if you have any type of internet connection, you know how to use it to find whatever resources (free or paid) that you need for learning your target language. If you don't have an internet connection, that's fine too. The materials in this book will be still be useful if you decide to use books or other written materials exclusively for self-study.

The objective of this book is not to **teach** you a specific language, but rather to help you design your own personalized study plan that works best for your schedule and language goals. It also provides insight as to why certain activities such as listening to music or learning grammar structures are better suited for language learners at certain levels, and explains simple yet effective strategies **for approaching these and other aspects of**

Introduction

language that are common sticking points for all language learners.

Specifically, this book includes proven strategies that will:

- Help you decide how to structure your language learning to your schedule
- Give you advice on how to choose the **right materials** to fit the level of the language that you possess
- Allow you to get the most out of the materials that you choose to study the language
- Provide ways to assess your progress along the way in order to know when you are ready to move to tougher materials
- Give you concrete exercises that **WILL** improve your proficiency with **ALL** modalities of your desired language (speaking, reading, writing, listening) not just speaking with the goal of fluency
- Tell you what **NOT** to do at certain points of your language training

This book is designed to help students of **ANY** language answer the question that many language learners ask themselves: "Where do I start?" or "How should I continue or refresh my knowledge of a language?" or "How should I organize my study time?" or "What should I do to practice my listening, writing, speaking, or reading?" If you've ever asked yourself any of these questions, wanted to learn a language for the first time, or wanted to improve your skills in a particular language, then there's something in this book for you.

Finally, from what I've seen outside of targeted military and government language training, most attempts to become proficient in a foreign language in a purely academic environment (even with school sponsored immersion trips, the inclusion of native speaker teachers, etc.) fail. I myself took 4 years of Japanese in college, to include a summer immersion trip to Japan and could barely say complete sentences outside of the ones that I had memorized to be able to pass my classes.

When it comes to becoming proficient in a language there are typically only three options:

1. Be raised in an environment where the language is spoken
2. Learn as an adult through constant exposure in an environment where the language is spoken, usually as a result of an organized program
3. Learn as an adult through sheer strength of will through self-study (take classes or study/practice on your own etc.)

While some people are fortunate to be born into option 1, or have the resources and connections to learn through option 2, most are forced to turn to option 3 as the only means to learn a language. That is where this book comes in.

What This Book Is

This book is a practical guide to learning a language that is designed to help you structure and focus your language studies.

I have divided language learners into five levels, listed below:

Introduction

- Level 1: Beginner (includes people who are "language interested")
- Level 2: Advanced Beginner
- Level 3: Intermediate
- Level 4: Advanced
- Level 5: Native-like

At each level, I include the specific activities that you should be focusing on while you study in that level.

More importantly, I include the things that you should **NOT** be focusing on at each level. This will help keep you focused on systematically improving and crawling before you walk so to speak.

What This Book Isn't

This book will not teach you a language!

This book does not talk in detail about specific language tools!

This is not a quick results book! Done properly, it may take you at least a year and a half or more to reach your goals from scratch, and that still depends on what your goals are, how much time you have available to study, and how dedicated you are to improving. If you have the same or similar ambition that I had to have an almost native like understanding and capability with a language, then that will obviously take longer. The techniques in this book must be adopted and practiced ideally daily with discipline in order to function properly.

Language Fluency vs. Language Literacy

Many language learning tools use **fluency** as the pinnacle of achievement when it comes to measuring the success of learners who use them.

While fluency can mean having overall mastery in any skill, in the context of foreign languages, it almost always refers to being able to **speak** the language well and clearly.

Of course speaking is crucial to communicating in a foreign language, but concentrating only on speaking fails to account for the other modalities of the language. Being able to understand it aurally (listening), understand it in written format (reading), and produce the language in writing (writing), are often left out of the **fluency** formula.

For this reason, in this book we will speak primarily of language **literacy** instead of fluency. It provides greater clarity towards the broader skill of being able to use the language in all modalities and in a wider variety of situations rather than simply being able to use it in conversations as a fluent language speaker.

Someone who can speak and understand English but can't read or write it would be considered illiterate. We are all illiterate in a foreign language when we begin to study it, which is completely understandable for a language that we have had little to no exposure to throughout the majority of our lives.

By expanding your definition of success in your target language from fluency or proficiency (which both often imply being good at speaking a language) to literacy, it will be easier for you to follow along with the suggestions in

Introduction

this book. This expanded definition is designed to include all modalities at all levels of literacy.

Getting Started (Chapter 1)

How to Use This Book (Students)

This book is not meant to be a "one and done" read. Rather it is meant to be a reference to help guide you through and structure your language studies. You may want to read through once initially it to get an idea of where you are going, but Chapters 2 through 6, are meant to be used to guide your language studies, and should be revisited as often as necessary. Chapter 7 is included to provide you with ways to turn your hobby into a career, by mentioning specific ways to make yourself more attractive to potential employers and clients. The final chapter outlines my hypothesis about the future of learning languages and how you can not only prepare for that future, but start to have an impact right now no matter what level of skill you possess in your target language.

If you—like many other language learners—are wondering where you should begin, then follow the below steps to receive the maximum benefit from this book.

Step 1: Determine Your Current Language Level through Self-Assessment

Assessing Your Language Skills

Assessing your language skills can be tricky business. If you try to speak with friends, family members, or native speakers, they will probably give you positive feedback, even if your skills are poor. Tutors are a little better, but they will often only be willing to provide feedback if you pay them more money.

The bottom line is that outside sources, as well-intentioned as they may be, are often unreliable sources for how proficient we are in a foreign language.

We need a more reliable way to self-assess our language skills. The most honest assessment comes when we examine how confident we are with the target language.

Language and Confidence

Being able to speak a language fluently or be literate in a language is a matter of confidence. Yes, it is true that knowledge of complex grammar concepts and a large vocabulary are helpful, but keep in mind that there are people who can speak and understand a language very well, but have little or no knowledge of grammar or have never cracked open a dictionary.

Think about when you speak your native language. Well, most of the time you don't have to think about it, because things just "sound correct" to you. Because of this you are, for the most part, 99% confident that you can convey any meaning that you want when you open your mouth.

Getting Started

However, when you speak a foreign language, this confidence level plummets. Suddenly, you have a hard time expressing yourself with even basic requests or statements and you struggle to pronounce words and form sentences. In other words, not only are you are not very confident that you can say what you mean, but also that someone else will be able to grasp that meaning.

Using a language that you have little knowledge in can be a frustrating and terrifying experience. Whether you are worried about not being understood from a survival perspective, or just simply being embarrassed by completely mutilating the language that you are attempting to speak, the underlying fear is the same: massive discomfort. Discomfort for you, and for anyone unfortunate enough to have to listen to you.

As you study and gain more exposure to the language, that confidence rises. Then eventually your confidence will be comparable to the confidence that you have in your native language.

The problem with confidence is that it can be difficult to assess accurately, especially when we are assessing ourselves. It is for this reason that I have designed the Language Confidence Scale (LCS). The LCS is meant to provide you with a Language Confidence Level (LCL), which will give you a better idea of how confident you feel when operating in another language. Ultimately, this will give you a quantifiable metric that will provide you with a better idea of where you stand with your chosen language. With that metric as a point of departure, it will be easier for you to answer one of the most difficult questions to answer when you decide to study a language: Where do I begin?

Tower of Babbling

What is the Language Confidence Scale (LCS)?

The LCS allows you to determine the level of language skill that you possess by answering 7 questions and rating yourself on them from a 0 to 5 point scale.

After you have answered all of the questions, you will determine your LCL. The LCL will help you pinpoint what part of the book you should begin using to improve your skills. Ask yourself these questions:

(Overall comfort with the language) How nervous do you feel when using the language in any modality? (0 - 5)

- 0 = I've never used the language to speak with anyone
- 1 = Very Nervous! I feel self-conscious and anxious anytime I use the language
- 2 = I can say a few words but worry about being able to understand responses from others that I receive in the target language.
- 3 = I can have short exchanges but have with family and close friends, but I have anxiety about being able to have a full conversation with people that I don't know.
- 4 = I am comfortable when using the language in my professional setting and with family and close

friends, but get nervous about using it in an unknown context.

5 = Not at all nervous, I feel comfortable using the language in most settings and situations

(Pronunciation) How accurate are you with the language? (0 - 5)

0 = I've never used the language to speak with anyone.
1 = Not accurate at all. I can't tell how accurate my pronunciation is
2 = I understand what accurate pronunciation sounds like, but it takes considerable effort to pronounce things correctly and I make mistakes often
3 = I understand what accurate pronunciation sounds like but it takes some effort to pronounce words correctly. I am aware that I make mistakes occasionally.
4 = I make very few pronunciation errors and I know how to self-correct most errors that I make.
5 = Very accurate, my pronunciation is native-speaker like.

(Grammar) How accurate are you with the language? (0 - 5)

0 = I've never used the language to communicate with anyone
1 = Not accurate at all. I can't tell how accurate my grammar is.
2 = I know several grammar concepts but I struggle to apply them in real time conversations.

3 = I understand what accurate grammar sounds like, but it takes effort to use what I know correctly, and I make mistakes often
4 = I make very few grammar errors, and I know how to self-correct most errors that I make.
5 = Very accurate, my grammar usage is native-speaker like.

(Speaking) How well do you feel like others can understand you when you speak the language? (0 - 5)

0 = I've never used the language to speak with anyone.
1 = Most people cannot understand me and they ask for clarification often.
2 = My family and close friends can understand me, but few people outside of my circle can understand me.
3 = I feel like I can perform day to day activities (non-work activities) and feel understood.
4 = I can use the language in a work setting and to perform day to day activities (non-work activities).
5 = People almost always understand me, most native speakers of the language can understand me.

(Listening) How well can you understand others using the language at a normal spoken speed? (0 - 5)

0 = I can't understand anything at all.
1 = I cannot understand most spoken language and I have to ask for clarification often for what was said.
2 = I can understand my family and close friends, but outside of those people I am lost.

Getting Started

 3 = I can understand speech necessary to perform day to day activities (non-work activities).
 4 = I can understand language related to my profession and language needed to perform day to day activities.
 5 = I understand almost everything that most people that speak the language say.

(Writing) How well can you write the language? (0 - 5)

 0 = I've never written/typed the language before.
 1 = I can't form a complete paragraph on my own or with the extensive help of an external source (dictionary, app, etc.).
 2 = I can form short sentences with the help of an external source, but writing takes considerable effort for me to communicate anything effectively.
 3 = I can form basic communications (non-work related) without the help of an external source.
 4 = I can form communications related to my profession and in everyday communications on my own, without the help of an external source.
 5 = I can fully express myself completely and accurately in almost any context, without the need for an external source.

(Reading) How well can you read the language? (0 - 5)

 0 = I've never tried to read more than single words in the language.
 1 = I can read single words, but can't understand a complete sentence. I use external sources (dictionaries, app, websites etc.) anytime I want to read in the target language.

2 = I can read complete sentences, and some paragraphs, but I struggle to understand the overall meaning of what I read. I heavily rely on external sources when I read.

3 = I can read and understand most text related to basic activities (non-work related) on my own. I occasionally use external sources to help me understand what I read.

4 = I can read and understand most text related to my profession and basic (non-work related) activities on my own. I rarely use external sources to help me understand what I read.

5 = I can read almost anything in the language without the aid of external sources.

These seven questions are designed to assess your personal opinion of your abilities in each of the major functions of a foreign language.

- Overall confidence with the language
- Pronunciation
- Grammar
- Speaking
- Listening
- Writing
- Reading

To determine your LCL, simply add your scores from each question, and compare the result to the list below. Your score will correspond to the section of this book that you should focus on. It will also point you in the right direction when it comes to seeking out other learning materials in your target language.

Getting Started

- LCL 0-7: Beginner
- LCL 8-14: Advanced Beginner
- LCL 15-18: Intermediate
- LCL 19-25: Advanced
- LCL 26+: Native-like

Now that you have a better idea of where you should begin, I encourage you to go the section of the book that corresponds to your LCL and read the "Who is…" section at the beginning of the chapter. This will provide a brief and general description of what you should be able to do with the language at that level. While it is not necessary to be able to perform all of the tasks in this section, comfort with **most** of them is a strong indicator that the level is a good fit for you.

እስቲ አስብ

Consider this: Remember, there is no such thing as perfection when speaking foreign languages. Native speakers make grammatical and pronunciation mistakes all the time. Some "mistakes" become so widely accepted that they form new words, dialects, accents, and even new languages. What matters is that a message that was conveyed was received and understood by its intended recipient, no matter how "ugly" or "incorrect" it may seem to you. Keep this in mind when assessing yourself, and be kind to yourself.

እስቲ አስብ

Step 2: Go To the Applicable Language Level of the Book and Read the Entire Chapter

In addition to the "✓ **Who is…**" section that begins chapters 2 - 6, each chapter contains the following sections:

- ✓ **Action Items**
- ✓ **Things to Avoid**
- ✓ **A Sample Study Plan**
- ✓ **Estimated Length of Time at Each Level**
- ✓ **How to Know When to Move On**
- ✓ **General Notes**
- ✓ **Quick Notes**

After you've assessed your language skills, I recommend going to (and reading) the entire chapter that matches your Language Confidence Level (LCL). After you've completed your read through then return to the "Action Items" section of the chapter to choose the elements of the language that you want to focus on. I will explain the contents of each section in detail below:

<u>Structure of Language Levels</u>

- **List of Action Items.** These are the specific activities that you should be focusing on in that chapter. You should focus on the action items that align with your goals for your target language.
- **Things to Avoid.** These are the things that you should make sure to avoid while you train yourself in that particular chapter. They are broken down by language modality beginning in the intermediate chapter.

Getting Started

- **Sample Study Plan.** A sample study plan is included in each chapter. These incorporate the action items at that particular level. The suggested time distributions are meant to reflect the percentage of your available study time that you should use on each action item. They are also provided to give you an idea of how to best optimize your available study time. The samples provided include all modalities of the language, but you **can and should** modify the plan to meet your unique goals and life situation.
- **Estimated Length of Time of Each Level.** The time assumes that you are studying for at least an hour a day at least 5 days a week. Of course you will progress faster if you are a full-time student and/or practice **every day**, but the time may be lengthened or shortened to account for your personal goals.
- **How to Know When to Move On.** This section outlines suggested criteria for evaluating your progress so that you know when to move on to more challenging materials in each level or move on to the next chapter.
  It is not necessary to be able to meet all of these requirements before you continue. However, progressing before you're ready will slow down your progress in the long run.
- **General Notes.** This includes general information about each level, that you should keep in mind as you study the chapter.
- **Quick Notes.** This is a summary of the major points of that chapter.

Step 3: Gather the Necessary Materials for Your Study Plan

This may include purchasing books, apps, software, and other tools or finding free resources online, in libraries etc. that you need to meet your language goals. If you can get materials for free, even better. But try to get everything as you begin each chapter, so that you don't have to interrupt the flow of your studies later on.

Step 4: Design Your Study Plan and Write It Down

Now you will design your personalized study plan based on your needs and goals.

I recommend confining your study plan to the "Action Items" in each chapter, or else you risk becoming overwhelmed with the amount of things that you need to learn.

Use the "Sample Study Plan" as a template for dividing up your time. The percentage of time dedicated to each activity is included to give you ideas of how you might break up your study time. You may use the template as is, or customize it to meet your needs.

Be sure to record your plan in some way, whether that means writing it down, taking a picture of it, typing it, or doing something else. As long as it's in a format that you can understand and one that helps you remember what you have to do every day.

This plan will become the staple of your daily study, so be as thorough and as specific with it as you need to be. For example: "Read a Spanish book every other day", is not as effective as "Read *Cien Años de Soledad* for 30 mins every other day."

Step 5: Track and Assess Your Progress And Repeat the Entire Process As Many Times as Necessary Until Your Goals Are Met

As you progress in the study of your target language, it can become difficult to know how much you have improved with the language. Sure there are a number of apps, software, and language programs with convenient methods for tracking all manner of metrics related to your progress. Examples of such measures might include how many words you've learned, amount of time you've studied, and other items, but outside of these, progress can be difficult to track. The problem becomes more apparent when you reach the intermediate level and begin consuming more content in the target language, which can be nearly impossible to track it **all of the time.**

This is why it is important to **track** and **assess** your studies as best as you can. Doing so will help you in the following ways:

- It helps save time by not repeatedly studying concepts that you have already covered
- It helps review vocabulary and expressions in order learn them faster and more effectively
- It helps move vocabulary from the passive to active category faster (explained more in Chapter 4: Intermediate)

Assessing Your Progress

I provide suggestions on how to assess your progress at the end of each chapter based on the skills that you should have at the beginning of the next chapter. However, here are some basic guidelines on **when** and **how** you should assess yourself:

How Often Should You Assess Your Performance (For Beginners And Advanced Beginners)

- You will generally make rapid progress at these levels. I suggest evaluating yourself **once a week** until you are able to advance to the intermediate level.

How Often Should You Assess Your Performance (For Intermediate Learners And Up)

- Notable progress at higher levels becomes much slower after you've mastered the basics of the language. Therefore, I recommend assessing your skills **once a month**, since you will probably not see much improvement from week to week at these levels.

Tracking Your Progress Using a Language Journal

- After you reach the Intermediate level, faithfully and consistently tracking your progress can be very difficult. The amount of vocabulary, idioms, cultural concepts, and other aspects of the language that you will encounter on a daily basis won't be easy to track.

Getting Started

- Therefore, I suggest keep a **language journal** to keep track of the activities that you do during your study time. Here's how you can do it:
    - **STEP 1**: Buy a notebook (or use a notepad app)
    - **STEP 2**: Write down the **activity** that you did that involved your language and **how long you did it**. Also take note of any new vocabulary, expressions, grammar concepts, etc. that you want learned from that activity.
    - **STEP 3**: Make time to review the contents of your journal during your study time at least once a week.
- Writing things down is helpful, but it will be even more helpful if you review what you wrote.
    - Keeping a language journal can not only help you organize the things that you are learning, but it also help put those things in the context of how you encountered them, which helps move information to your long-term memory faster.

How to Use This Book (For Language Teachers / Instructors)

Although this book was written for the purpose of helping students of languages study on their own, it can still be a very useful tool in a formal study environment. If you teach languages, you will be able to more actively track the progress of your students within each level, and help guide them toward activities that will strengthen areas that they may be struggling with.

Using the Language Journal

I recommend using the language journal as a graded item. Have the students consistently mark things in their language journal that they want to work on or should work on outside of class. At fixed or random intervals, check with them to see how they are learning the language outside of class. Use the content (or lack of content) in their language journal to advise them on how to improve their language skills.

Designing Assignments (In And Out Of Class)

You can and should design assignments around the "Action Items" in each chapter. They are designed to focus on each aspect of the language individually (listening, speaking, writing, and reading) so students will be able to focus on one area at a time without becoming too overwhelmed.

Helping With Self-Assessments

The items in the "How to Know When to Move On" sections in each chapter can easily be converted into graded tests and quizzes.

Use them to further gauge the student's progression and help you identify areas that are weaknesses for them.

A Self-Study Mindset

Studying to become literate in a foreign language can be a daunting task. That's why it is absolutely important to have a clear goal in mind before you get started.

What is your why? Is it to get a job? To be able to get in better touch with distant or close relatives? Or do you just want an intellectual challenge?

Defining your "why" early on will not only help keep you on track when things get difficult and frustrating, but it will also help you know what types of materials you want to study with and which ones will waste your time.

All of the advice in this book will be helpful for you only if you are willing to work hard and meet your goals.

I have been that person who was intimidated by the flood of unfamiliar sounds that was supposed to be another language and thought, "This is impossible, I'll never be able to understand this." I've also persevered through my own doubt and frustration, in order to not only to understand and communicate using the language, but also to be a more globally aware and connected human being.

This level of achievement is waiting for you as well. If you cultivate the correct mindset and gather the right tools that best suit your needs, this book will help push you the rest of the way towards making your dreams come true with your language.

A Note for Heritage Language Learners

Learning a language can be a humbling experience for anyone, but for those who have a heritage language that for one reason or another they never learned very well when they were children, it can be a particularly emotional topic. This is because often, the language is so closely tied to family tradition, values, and identity that a student may feel disconnected from their family or (even worse) a part of themselves, because they can't speak the language. This leads them to feel a sense of embarrassment or shame about their lack of language skills.

While I am not a heritage speaker of any language, I do know many people who are. From talking to them about it, I know that some of them feel somehow inadequate that they even have to study the language, because they think they should have made more of an effort to learn it when they were younger.

If you are a language learner with a heritage language, know that whether you haven't learned the language 1) because your parents made the conscious choice not to teach you or 2) because back then you had no interest to do so is irrelevant. What **does** matter is that you are willing to learn now, and the fact that you are reading this book means that you have taken a step in the right direction to learn it and reconnect with your roots. It also means that it probably won't take as much time for you to reach your language goals, compared with a student who has had no exposure to the language.

A Final Note for Experienced Language Learners

If you, like me, have years or decades of experience learning or teaching languages, first of all thank you for reading my book. I hope you are able to extract at least a little bit of value from it. Additionally, I am aware that there are multiple ways, methods, and best practices for achieving what most of us ultimately want, which is to be able to understand and/or communicate in a language other than the one(s) that we were exposed to as children.

That being said, while you may disagree with the sequence or exact way that I propose students use certain exercises or techniques for learning their language, know that like any other person who has written a book of this nature, the activities are based on my personal experiences learning languages. There is no way that I could possibly cover EVERY possible approach or theory for the "best" way to learn a language and I doubt you or anyone else could either. Also, as you know, the word "best" is very subjective when it comes to this field, and greatly depends on a student's learning style, available study time, and unique goals.

What are presented throughout this book are **some** ways that have certainly been effective for me and many other people over the years, and my hope is that it makes the entire process of learning one or multiple languages feel possible for someone who has considered adopting that goal, but has never been able to fully realize it.

In short, this book was ultimately not intended for someone who has already found their own uniquely successful system for becoming literate in any language. If you have had success in becoming fluent, proficient, or completely literate to a collegiate native speaker level in one or multiple languages using techniques and suggestions that I don't recommend or mention, then I am happy for your achievement. By all means continue to do what works for you. As we say where I'm from "there's more than one way to skin a cat", and I am fully aware that the techniques that I outline may be contrary to yours and you might not completely agree with the approach that I propose.

If you, however, are willing to indulge me just a little, you might just find a new way to look at how you approach language learning in order to arrive at the same destination where most of us want to go, which is the ability to express ourselves completely in another language.

Beginner Level (Chapter 2)

This is where all foreign language learners start. It begins with a desire to want to finally understand what those people were saying, get a better job, or just to satisfy that curiosity. These are some of the reasons that drive us to sign up for the first class, join the Meetup group, or watch the YouTube videos, in order to take those first stumbles into a new language. It's an exciting time, and you never know where a new language will take you. It could lead to unforgettable travel opportunities, that dream job, or even a long lasting relationship. The best thing about it is that there is no requirement necessary to begin, and anyone can do it, even you!

Who Is A Beginner Learner?

Anyone interested in learning a language! No skills or prior exposure necessary!

Action Items for Beginners

Find One or Two Tools to Learn the Language

There are countless numbers of tools available to learn a language. The tool can be anything: books, apps, podcasts, classes (on and offline), tutors, friends who speak the language, etc.

How to do it: Choose one or two and **commit** to using it/them.

Research the Language

It can take years to become proficient in a language, so it's important that you **like** the language that you choose to learn.

Do you like the way the language sounds? Do you like certain media in that language? Or traveling to places where the language is spoken? What do you think about the culture of the language and its people?

These are all important things to consider **before** you decide to commit what could be a large amount of time with this language, its people and culture.

How to do it: Watch short videos or listen to short dialogues about the language

Talk to people that you know about the language (natives of the culture, other students, teachers etc.) and ask them questions about it.

Beginner Level

Pay attention to what your first impressions of the language are. Ask yourself if you want to commit to studying it for a year or longer.

Have Fun With It!

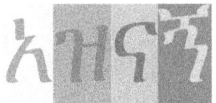 When you begin learning a language, naturally you will want to show off the few words and phrases that you know.

You should make sure to do that in order to build up your enthusiasm for the language. That enthusiasm will help drive you to form a concrete study plan and progress to the Advanced Beginner level.

How to do it: Show off your skills to friends/family at every opportunity

Things to Avoid: Beginners

Being a new learner of a language can be a lot of fun. On the other hand, it can be easy to sabotage your confidence level and skills even at this early phase. Avoid doing the following things as a beginner:

Do not use/listen to/watch etc. materials designed for native speakers to learn the language (yet). I know many people learn languages to be able to consume media in their target language (i.e. learning Japanese to watch Anime), but you won't be able to learn much from these materials at this point, even if you are watching with subtitles in your native language. Stay away for now.

Don't expect to have perfect pronunciation and grammar usage when you speak. This curse can affect many of you perfectionists out there. Of course, your Mandarin doesn't sound like it *should* when you first begin to speak it. It will take much more exposure and experience with the language to make it sound like native level Mandarin. The point at this level is just to talk as much as possible! Don't worry about what it sounds like.

Avoid using too many language tools at the same time. I've been guilty of this too often. When I first decided to learn Spanish I was so excited that I bought 5 books about how to learn Spanish, including one that was all in Spanish. I did the same with Japanese many years ago. Two things happened in both instances when I looked at the pile of books and thought about where I should begin: 1) I became completely overwhelmed by all of the materials that I had and 2) I couldn't use them because they were too advanced. The result was that I never opened some of those books at all and just seeing them collect dust on a shelf made me feel foolish for ever wanting to even try to learn the language.

Try to stick with no more than two tools until you have almost or completely finished them. You will get more out of the materials that way.

Don't spend too much time reading or watching materials <u>about</u> the language, instead of actually <u>learning</u> it. In the 21st century, the amount of content about a foreign language almost seems to rival the amount of useful materials about how to learn the concepts of the language. An example of this might be listening to recordings or watching videos of people who became proficient with the language. Or you might be distracted by other cultural aspects of the language—by watching endless Japanese dramas, for example, but not focusing on the actual Japanese.

In the beginning it's better to use your time speaking simple sentences than it is listening to others who already speak the language or watching other videos that will not help you learn the language.

Sample Study Plan for Beginners

Completing activities in your language learning tool: 70%

- Due the abundant number of options available today for learning a language, it's important that the tools that you choose be **fun and engaging** for you. Make sure it is something that you wouldn't mind going back to again and again during the early phases of your language learning.
- Of course the tool should also **include audio** (preferably with native speakers) and **fit within your budget.**

Learning General Information about the language: 20%

- **Look for videos, articles, etc.** about the language to find out if you truly want to invest the time to become proficient in it. Making time to do this now may save you effort and money in the long run.

Show off your new skills to friends/family! 10%

- At this point you won't be able to say much, but the little that you do know WILL impress people that don't know the language. So **have fun with it!**

Estimated Length Of Time At The Beginner Level?

- 1 day - 1 month
- The reality is that, most people who begin to study or resume studying a language have probably had interest in that culture or language for some time. So the time spent in the beginner phase will be minimal. The amount of time here is completely dependent on the person's desire to get serious about setting goals and deliberately studying or practicing the language.

How to Know When to Move On To the Next Level

You will no longer be a beginner with the language after:

- You've done your initial research on the language and decided you still want to study it
- You are ready to commit to really **studying** the language, not just casually visiting it when you have free time available
- You have a clear goal for **why** you want to learn the language
- You have established a **general timeline** for when you want to reach your language goal

General Notes on the Beginner Level

It's no secret that many people don't make it past the beginner phase of language learning. Why does this happen?

Beginner Level

- The first reason is that most language learners had no passion for the language that they studied. Many of us were forced to take a language class during our school days, and after completing the classes, could barely hold a basic conversation. As a result, we felt like we were bad at learning languages and carried that stigma around for the rest of our lives, even when we tried again to learn as adults.
- Another reason people stop as Beginners is because the foreign language market is saturated with tools across all mediums for teaching beginners a foreign language, and language students are overwhelmed by the amount of materials available to learn a language. Most of these tools market themselves as "the only program that you need to become fluent", but the reality is that few of them are designed to take students beyond the basics of the language. This further discourages students to continue their studies after they finish using the tool and find that they have not achieved the fluency promised.
- Finally, there are few language learning tools designed for intermediate and advanced learners. This means that even those few students who do work through all of the basic materials have no idea how to take their skills to the next level, so the majority give up altogether.

How to Avoid Giving Up

Focusing on **the reason why you want to learn** and **having a concrete plan** are the easiest ways to avoid falling into the category of those who began learning a language but quit early on in the process. This book will help you form the plan. But you have to come up with your reason why and hold yourself to it, because few other people will.

Beginner Level Quick Notes

DO

- Find one or two tools to learn the language AND FOCUS YOUR ATTENTION PRIMARILY ON COMPLETING THEM!
- Research the potential target language
- Have fun speaking!

DON'T

- Use/listen/watch materials designed for native speakers
- Expect to have perfect pronunciation and grammar usage when you speak
- Use too many language tools at the same time
- Spend too much time reading/watching materials <u>about</u> the language. (Focus on practice and learning)

Advanced Beginner Level
(Chapter 3)

So you've finally decided that this is the year that you are going to take that backpacking trip through the French Alps and it's time to get serious about picking up some French. You set the date on your calendar for September, so that gives you nine months to learn a decent amount of the language so that you can get around a little better in the country, absorb more of the culture, and impress any native French speakers that you encounter along the way. Welcome to the Advanced Beginner level! This is the level defined less by skill with the language and more by the desire to learn it in concrete way, in order to meet a specific goal.

Who Is An Advanced Beginner?

A person who <u>actively studies</u> the language in a structured way.

Someone who creates a realistic language study plan using their available time and target finish date as a guide.

Action Items for Advanced Beginners

Find a trustworthy bilingual dictionary

- Try to find a general bilingual dictionary to start. Some dictionaries include commonly used phrases in the language, which can be helpful if you plan to use the language right away.
- Pocket dictionaries can be convenient and portable. Online dictionaries are powerful resources, but be sure it has an offline mode or you may be screwed if you go somewhere without an internet connection.

Find a reliable grammar resource

- The grammar resource should cover the major aspects of grammar in the language. It doesn't matter if it includes drills or exercises (though most will). The drills may be helpful to reinforce certain aspects of the grammar, but for the most part you can rely on exposure to the language to pick up the grammar intuitively.
- **Don't dive into the grammar book right now.** Just have it on hand to use as a reference for now. You'll come back to it later as you gain more exposure to the language.

Learn the basic phonetics and sounds of your language

- This is where the real work begins for your new language. You will have to start slowly to **sound out**

words just like you did in your early school days. You also need to **train your** ear to recognize certain sounds that are different from your native language.
- The easiest way to do this is to find recordings and explanations online that you can listen to and imitate, until you learn to produce and understand the sounds naturally.

Begin to deliberately study the writing system of the language

- Being able to write in a foreign language is something that many language learners often overlook. However, being able to understand the basic writing system will give you access to native level materials later on in your studies. For some languages like Japanese, you will have to learn the more complex writing system if you hope to ever read authentic materials. Therefore, it's important that you learn to recognize the foreign script of your target language, especially if it is very different from your native language.
- Most grammar books will have the basics of the writing system, but for languages like Japanese, Chinese, and others that have more complex writing systems, you may have to find a separate resource for learning the script.

Begin to read short and easy dialogues in your language

- Reading can be intimidating at first, but by starting small (one sentence at a time) you will build up quickly.
- You will probably get some reading practice with your language tool, so you won't have to go out of your way to find practice materials at first.
- Search online for anything with your language and keywords like:
    - "reading for beginners"
    - "reading for kids"
    - "easy reading" etc.
- From these searches you should be able to find materials suitable for your level.
- ALWAYS read out loud if possible, even if your pronunciation is terrible in the beginning, and don't stress about the unknown vocabulary or grammar at this point.
- Begin to listen to short, easy and slow dialogues in your language

    Listening practice is easy to find at this level largely because you will be getting so much of it from your language tool.

    If you are looking for more practice, follow the same advice stated above: Search online for anything with your language and keywords like "listening for beginners" "listening for kids", "easy listening" "slow listening" etc. and you should be able to find materials suitable for your level.

With any of the materials that you choose make sure that you can understand at least **70%** of it. If you can't understand at least that much, you will most likely not benefit much from it, because your brain will just filter it out. On the other hand, if you understand 100% of what you're listening to, then obviously you won't be learning anything from that either.

Consider getting a tutor

Just because you are learning a language on your own doesn't mean that you have to do it alone. Working with a tutor can help you in the following ways:

- Tracking and evaluating your progress
- Helping you with problem areas in your pronunciation
- Providing cultural insight and context to the language
- Motivating you to continue with your studies

Hiring a tutor can come with its own series of potential issues. We will discuss each of the potential obstacles and ways to avoid them in detail below.

OBSTACLE: **COST.** 1-on-1 tutoring can be expensive. The more established the tutor the more expensive the sessions. If you decide to go the budget-tutor route in order to save money, you may not receive quality instruction.

SOLUTION: **BUDGET A FIXED AMOUNT** that you are willing to spend on a tutor and check their rates to ensure that they are compatible with your budget.

OBSTACLE: **EFFECTIVENESS OF TUTORS.** Anyone can become a tutor nowadays with an internet connection. It can be difficult to know which ones are quality and which ones will waste your time.

SOLUTION: **DO YOUR RESEARCH AHEAD OF TIME** and check for favorable ratings and student feedback, before you proceed to book your first lesson. Most tutors offer a trial session for free, be sure to use this option to see if the tutor's style and personality fit well with your goals.

OBSTACLE: **TUTORING SESSIONS WITH NO GOALS.** The first few times you meet with a tutor can be very awkward and intimidating. What will you talk about? How will you say it with your limited vocabulary? Will you get along with your tutor? All of these questions and more can make you question if you made the right decision to hire a tutor in the first place. Here are some ways to maximize sessions with tutors. These can also be applied to live in-person classes or group sessions online.

SOLUTION: **THINK ABOUT WHAT YOU SPECIFICALLY WANT HELP WITH BEFORE THE TUTORING SESSION.** This will help keep your sessions focused and on target. For example, if you want to discuss a certain piece of material online with the tutor or use it as a reading exercise, look it up ahead of time to save yourself time during the session. Below are some possible topics that you could ask about during the tutoring session:

Certain grammar concepts

New words and expressions that you've encountered

Cultural questions

Current events

Advanced Beginner Level

You should try to speak as much as possible. Don't let the tutor just talk the entire time. Respectfully and politely try and work your way into the conversation as much as you can. **_IF YOU CAN'T COME UP WITH THINGS TO SAY IN YOUR TARGET LANGUAGE, ASK YOUR TUTOR HOW TO SAY WHAT YOU WANT TO SAY, AND REPEAT WHAT THEY TELL YOU_.** Make sure to ask for feedback on what you said.

Try to only use your target language. This is difficult in the beginning when you can barely form sentences, but it gives you valuable practice. It also gives the tutor more to work with, because they will be able to help you with problems with pronunciation or word usage that you may be struggling with.

Do your homework (if there is any). Few people like doing homework, but if you are serious about learning your language, you should make time for it. It shows the tutor that you are serious about learning the language, which will make them more eager to help you improve. It also helps you apply what you learned during the lesson, which will help you learn it that much faster.

Form a good relationship with your tutor. Hiring a tutor can be a great way to form a relationship with someone who speaks your target language. This is especially true if it's a 1-on-1 session, since you should have the tutor's undivided attention for at least an hour.

The better you know your tutor the more informal they will be with you, and that will make it easier to learn more casual forms of speech and make the sessions that much more enjoyable.

Resist the urge to change tutors (if you can help it). With the number of options available it can be tempting to switch tutors to adapt to your schedule or to find a better rate any time things get inconvenient. This can be problematic because with every new tutor there will inevitably be an adjustment to that person's style and manner that may take a few lessons; this will only make it more difficult to focus on your primary goal of improving with the language...

...Therefore, after you have shopped around, do your best to stay with that tutor as long as your schedule and budget will allow. In this way, you will be able to focus on improving your language skills instead of trying to constantly adapt to the styles and personalities of several tutors.

Be open to feedback and correction with your language. One of the best things about having a tutor is the ability to receive feedback on your performance with the language. However, you must humble yourself to be able to receive feedback constructively from them. It can be vexing to be constantly interrupted and corrected by someone who may be younger or have more experience with the language than you do.

Set your ego aside and try not to get frustrated. Remind yourself that every mistake is making you better at speaking the language, and having a tutor to point them out helps you correct them much faster than if you were on your own.

Things to Avoid: Advanced Beginners

Purchasing or starting other language tools that go over the basics of the language (you are not a beginner anymore). By the time you have been an Advanced

Advanced Beginner Level

Beginner for at least a month or two, you will probably begin to notice the limits of the language tool that you chose to use initially. You will have completed most of the lessons and will be looking for ways to continue your studies. It is at this point where it can be tempting to purchase or seek out another similar language tool for this purpose. **DO NOT DO THIS!**

As I stated before, most language tools are not designed to push you beyond the beginner or intermediate level of a language. Buying another tool will most likely not help you progress very much, in fact, it may **harm** your progress, by distracting you with materials that you are already familiar with.

We like tools, apps, and courses because they provide us a sense of direction and security within the confines of their programs. This need for direction can keep you going in circles with your progress. Trust me. It's happened to me too many times to count.

As you begin to approach the Intermediate level, you need to have faith in yourself and your plan and begin to build your own path to your language goals.

Neglecting to learn the writing system. Many language learners often ignore the writing system in their language because their focus tends to be on being able to speak and understand the language well. However, this often proves to be a poor choice after they realize that they can't consume many materials created for native speakers of the language. This happened to me with Japanese. The first time that I looked at a Japanese newspaper after 3 years of studying the language, I was floored by the amount of kanji characters that I needed to know. Don't let this happen to you.

Focusing on studying grammar. It can be irritating not knowing how to express basic concepts in your target language, so this leads to the temptation to look up in a dictionary or elsewhere how to work with certain grammatical structures, generally too early in the language learning process. For this reason, many new language learners both fear and love learning the grammar of a language. It's difficult to learn, but at the same time the desire to be able to say anything correctly can make us want to look up grammar from day one. Knowing grammar is important, but endlessly drilling grammar concepts is an easy way to get bored with studying the language, especially if you do this too early on in the process.

- Believe it or not, by listening, reading, and speaking you will begin to pick up the grammar intuitively. I will discuss grammar acquisition more in-depth in the next chapter, but for now, you should not focus on studying grammar. Without the necessary amount of context and exposure, you will quickly forget the grammar that you are exposed to and make it more difficult to express yourself in the language, because you will focus more on making your speech more grammatically correct than just speaking. Do yourself a favor and save grammar for later.

Waiting until you "know" the language to speak it
Leaving behind the safety of our native language to attempt to speak another can be a terrifying experience. In one language you can express any feeling or desire that you can think of and in the other, you can barely convey

basic concepts about your identity. This universal experience that all people who speak a foreign language go through, is made worse by the initial reactions that people often respond with when they hear you speak for the first time. These reactions can range from laughter and ridicule, to scathing criticism or even indignation at how poor your pronunciation and grammar is.

The factors above can make us want to make sure that anything that comes out of our mouths in the foreign language, represents the native speaker version of what we are trying to convey. This is one of the worst ways I know to sabotage yourself when you are trying to learn how to speak the language. **You need to speak as much as possible to improve your ability to speak. Don't worry about trying to say things perfectly. Your pronunciation will improve as you expose yourself to more of the language. Don't let critics or haters stop you from getting the practice you need.**

Memorizing vocab lists. When you begin to study a language, vocabulary lists seem to be everywhere. On one hand, the lists are a convenient consolidation of terms that are usually related to a single topic (for example "Household items" or "Going shopping" or "Colors"). While this thematic approach to learning vocabulary can be beneficial, placing too much emphasis on it early on can be a distraction if you do not have an immediate need for those words. **Simply put, you will most likely forget most of the words that you learn from vocabulary lists.**

I will cover vocabulary acquisition in more detail in the next chapter, but for now just know to avoid rote memorization of terms if possible. This is what the majority of us were forced to do in school when we were learning our first foreign language. I don't know about you, but I hardly remember any of the words that I learned for those classes, so this clearly was not very effective back then and it won't be any more effective now.

Being too hard on yourself - Learning a language is like constructing a building, it takes time until it is erected and fit for public use. If you want to build a strong building, start by setting realistic expectations and goals for yourself. Being able to speak like a native speaker with no accent after 6 months or even a year of studying is not a realistic expectation. Go at your own pace, and give yourself room to grow as you absorb more of the language.

Remind yourself that you are building your skills, and with continued practice and patience you will reach your goals at some point in the future.

Sample Study Plans for Advanced Beginners

If you try to improve all aspects of your language at once, you will surely be overwhelmed by the amount of time you spend studying.

Therefore, I recommend breaking your available study time up into a two-day schedule that alternates. Every other day, you will program one set of activities for yourself, then tackle the other set of action items the next day. Below is an example of this alternate day schedule.

The percentages represent the the portion of available time that you have for learning the language.

For example: If you can only commit 1 hour a day to your

language studies, then a (50%) means that you would spend 30 minutes on that activity.

Two day schedule (alternate days)

Day 1

- **Language tool study** (focusing on pronunciation and ear training at first): **50%**
- **Language writing system** practice: **25%**
- **Reading short dialogues**: **25%**

Day 2

- **Listening** to short/slow/simple recordings: **50%**
- **Language tutor** (If you have one, if you don't have one, then replace with one of the above activities): **50%**

Estimated Length Of Time At The Advanced Beginner Level?

Approximately 3 - 6 months

This will be your first real experience committing to your self-study plan. You will probably begin with enthusiasm and excitement towards finally being able to realize a goal that perhaps you have put off for a long time. It is possible to use that momentum to see massive improvement quickly during this phase. If that is the case, you can possibly move on to the Intermediate level in as little as 3 months, but it will likely take most people longer to learn the basic essentials of their language.

If you are moving at a more modest pace, and have many other commitments like family, work, etc. your progress may be slower. That's fine. The important thing is to make sure you get some practice in every day if possible. Even 15 minutes a day during a lunch break or after the kids are asleep can make a difference overtime.

Remember, this time estimate assumes that you are starting the language from zero. Obviously, if you've taken classes in the language in school, or have a heritage language that you grew up hearing at home, then your progress will be much faster.

How to Know When to Move On To the Next Level

This is the first level in which the decision to advance to the next tier isn't very clear and will depend heavily on you being honest with yourself about the level of effort that you have put into your practice and studies. It will be the same for the rest of the levels from now on.

(Technically, I have been studying Japanese for 14 years, but that time has not been consistent, intentional, or measurable at all. Even with all of that exposure and time with the language, currently my Japanese is intermediate at best.)

The point is, the amount of time that you have studied a language is not a strong indicator of your skill with it. What matters is the amount of effort and attention that you have put into it. Only you can know how intentional you have been, and thus only you can tell yourself when you are truly ready to move on when you are studying on your own.

With that said, here are some ways to tell that you are ready to advance to the Intermediate level:

- You have learned the basic elements of the writing system (varies by language)
- You have an LCL of at least **18/35** [Refer to the explanation in the Getting Started (Chapter 1)]
- You have completely finished **at least one** language tool from the Beginner level
- You are ready to seriously invest more time and effort into learning the language

General Notes on the Advanced Beginner Level

You are officially a student of your language now so try to remain diligent and find time to study every day.

Actively look for opportunities to use/practice the language **outside** of your study time! This will give you confidence with your progress and help you improve faster.

Advanced Beginner Level Quick Notes

DO

- Find a bilingual dictionary
- Find a grammar resource
- Focus on learning to <u>produce</u> sounds that are different from your native language
- Focus on learning to <u>recognize</u> sounds that are different from your native language
- Study the writing system of the language
- Read short and easy content in your language
- Listen to short, easy and slow dialogues in your language

- Consider getting a tutor

DON'T

- Purchase or start another language tool that goes over the basics of the language. (You're not a beginner anymore)
- Neglect to learn the writing system
- Focus on studying grammar
- Wait until you "know" the language to speak it
- Memorize vocab lists
- Be too hard on yourself

Intermediate Level (Chapter 4)

It's been a few months since you decided to start relearning Chinese. Your parents and relatives spoke it often when you were young and you had a few lessons throughout elementary and middle school, but you could never speak or read it well. This time you were determined to learn. In 7 months you have completed an entire online Chinese course, 20 lessons with a tutor on italki.com, and hundreds of Chinese character flashcards in Anki. But you don't feel like you're getting anywhere.

Last week a friendly waitress struck up a conversation with you at a local Chinese restaurant, and you could barely have a basic conversation. You're confused about how to continue improving, and have even thought about giving up altogether. You can always use the latest translation technology that provides decent enough translations anyway.

This is a classic profile of an intermediate level language learner. In this chapter, we'll discuss some of the common pitfalls on this level that can keep you going in circles with your studies, and more importantly, how you can break the cycle in order to move on and achieve your language goals.

Who Is An Intermediate Learner?

A person who can understand basic written and spoken materials in the language.

Someone who strives to transition from beginner materials to materials designed by native speakers.

A student who can speak using simple sentences and general utterances.

Action Items for Intermediate Learners: Vocabulary

Create a plan for building your vocabulary

- As an intermediate learner, it is now time for you to start deliberately building your vocabulary. But what is the best way to do this?
- There is no easy answer to that question. A quick search online will show you that there are numerous methods to learn and retain vocabulary in your target language, all with various pros and cons attached to them.
- I will cover a few of the methods that I have experimented with over the years and discuss what I liked or did not like about them. Ultimately, it is up to you to choose a method to use and most importantly, **stick to it**. The earlier in your studies that you design a reliable and effective system for capturing new words, the more words that you will be able to call upon actively when you want to use them to communicate in your language.

Intermediate Level

The Trouble with Vocabulary

One of the frustrating aspects of learning new vocabulary is how we can easily lie to ourselves about how well we know or don't know a specific term.

Consider the following example: I take a Japanese class for adults and I have a vocabulary test coming up on 20 new terms. I study the terms the night before the test, wake up the next morning and score 100% on it. Now I **think** that I have memorized these terms because I was able to pass the test. Unfortunately, in reality, there's no way that I would probably be able to recognize any of the words within the context of written material, understand when a native speaker uses them, or produce the words in a real time conversation.

Many of you have probably experienced this same issue with learning vocabulary. It can be frustrating, because you don't know how to learn the terms in a way that not only allows you to recognize them in written and spoken form, but also allows you to produce them when you speak.

As monumental of a task that learning hundreds or thousands of vocabulary words in a foreign language may seem, it can be done! Yes even by you! The first thing that you need to do is change how you think about vocabulary words.

The Levels of Vocabulary

The way most of us think about vocabulary tends to be fairly linear. We think that either we know what a word means or we don't. For example, Take the Spanish word "pared" which means "wall" in English. You probably thought about the word and either you knew it or you didn't. End of story. This is how most of us think of words in a foreign language, but this binary approach fails to account for the **level of proficiency** that we actually have with the word. Even if I can see the word "pared" in this book and know it's definition, doesn't mean that I can always use it properly in a conversation or understand it being used in a context outside of a vocabulary test.

Let's begin to think of our knowledge of vocabulary in three levels of proficiency. These levels are as follows:

Level 3
Long term storage - Active Vocabulary) - You can recognize the word in most contexts and say it on demand.

Level 2
(Recognition - Passive Vocabulary) - You can recognize the word when you see it or hear it, but you don't know it well enough to say it without some effort.

Level 1
(Memorized Proficiency) - This is the level that most of us reach with the words that we learn in an academic environment. You may memorize them long enough to pass a test, but you can't recognize them in any other form (written or spoken).

Intermediate Level

Depending on your language goals, having most of your vocabulary in the passive category would be sufficient enough for getting by. But if you have plans to ever speak the language fluently, you should strive for most terms that you learn to make their way to your active vocabulary. As an interpreting instructor of mine once said, "you must **own** the word."

To truly own words, you should understand how to get the most out of your memory. Even if you think your memory is poor, I would bet that there are certain important events big or small that you can recall that may have happened 5, 10, or 15 years ago without much effort. To become better owners of words, we need to become more aware of not just the word, but the elements and circumstances that surround it.

Mastering Your Memory

When I made the decision to become literate in Spanish, I thought a lot about vocabulary. In fact, I was so fixated on building my vocabulary that my skill in the other modalities of the language suffered. After months of trial and error and research online, I finally figured out the winning formula that helped me learn and place several new words a day on their way to my brain's long-term storage.

The key to learning large amounts of vocabulary words and coding them to the long-term storage in your brain is ensuring that any vocabulary system that you use has some, if not, all of the elements listed below.

- **Context.** Learning words in context, not only helps you remember the words, but it also will tell you **when** is the best time to use them. For example, I'm much more likely to remember the word "gato" means "cat" in Spanish if I read a story about cats, than if I try and memorize the word from a vocabulary list of house pets in Spanish.
- **Repetition.** To truly "own" new words, you will most likely have to repeat and hear them being repeated a lot. That's how our minds work. The more we hear something repeated, the more important it will seem to our brain, therefore, we will have a greater chance of remembering it.
- **Pictures.** When we first encounter certain words in our target language, they are nothing but sounds and letters. They have no relevance to our current knowledge and we will most likely forget them. But if that same word is paired with a picture, it will be easier to link the word to a concept or words that we already know, which will help us remember it more easily. This is why learning words with books is so powerful, because your mind is already forming pictures to describe what you are reading and this helps you encode the word faster and hold onto it longer.
- **Audio.** You learned your native language by imitating the sounds that your parents and the people around you made. You will do the same for your target language. Having an audio sample that you can imitate will allow you to practice the correct intonation, pronunciation, and stress that is necessary to produce the words correctly. Without this element, it is possible to learn how to say words incorrectly,

which can be a difficult problem to correct with the passage of time.
- **Emotion.** Have you ever wondered why some of the first words that we seem to encounter in a foreign language seem to be expletives, curse words, and insults? For one, these words and expressions are usually easy to pronounce and remember. Another reason is that they tend to be used during moments of stress or heightened emotion, which make them hard to forget after you've encountered them in this context. While I don't recommend getting very angry or upset every time you want to memorize a new word in your target language, you should know that you will remember words much more easily if it is in an emotional context or linked to a specific emotion.
- **Kinesthetic Application.** Movement is another powerful element that can improve your chances of recalling new vocabulary. I am a big advocate of this element, and I have at least 4 college-ruled spiral notebooks filled with Spanish words to prove it. Writing is not the only way to take advantage of this kinesthetic element. You can also review words while walking, running, or doing any other number of activities to boost your chances of retaining the words.
- These elements, **context, repetition, pictures, audio, emotion,** and **kinesthetic application** are the keys to bulletproof vocabulary acquisition.

It may seem like too much work to bring all of these elements together **every time** that you want to learn a new word to mastery. Luckily, with modern technology, most of the work can be done for you. There are several apps, like Anki, and programs that allow you create your own flashcards that utilize spaced repetition systems and allow you add audio, pictures, and anything else you might need to learn new words. Many of these tools streamline the vocabulary process and will allow you to learn large amounts of words quickly. However, keep in mind that the process of searching the meaning of, and bringing all of the aforementioned elements together in and of itself will aid your retention of the word. On some occasions it may be beneficial to forego the fancy apps and dig around online to grasp even deeper meanings of the words that you are searching for.

Technology can be a powerful tool in learning vocabulary, but it can't account for the emotional and kinesthetic variables that aid memory retention. For that, you'll have to get creative by using any one of the methods we'll discuss next.

Vocabulary Methods

I will briefly list some of the vocabulary methods that I have tried out over the years, and lay out the pros and cons of each one. This will give you a better idea of what methods might work best for you and your learning style.

- **Paper Flashcards.** People have used paper flashcards for hundreds of years to drill vocabulary. It is an effective method that still works today. Flash cards are portable and you can customize them to meet your needs. Additionally, the work that you put into making the flashcard will help you remember the terms. The obvious disadvantage is that they don't contain any audio, and unless you are an artist

Intermediate Level

it can be difficult and time consuming to include pictures. Finally, carrying around around hundreds of flashcards can become quite cumbersome, so you will have to be mindful of the words that you really want to improve on.

- **Anki flashcards.** I mention a specific tool here only because at the time of this writing, it is one of the most popular and powerful examples of spaced repetition tools. Anki allows you to program your own flashcards with essentially anything you would need to learn the words. Below are some of the things that I programmed into my flashcards when I used it:
    o   Audio (Anki has text to speech audio)
    o   Image files from online
    o   Application cards (that allowed me to test my knowledge of the words)

Despite all of its advantages, Anki can have a pretty steep learning curve for a casual user. It may take some time to set it up properly so that it will meet your personal needs. However, if you manage to leverage it correctly, you will have one of the most powerful vocabulary learning machines available.

- **Writing words down AND reviewing them.** This is a simple and effective method that I still use to this day. By writing a word down, you engage the kinesthetic part of your brain, which aids retention. Over time you will create a personalized glossary of words that you have encountered, which is far better than finding stock glossaries online made by others, full of words that you have not encountered in context. **Be warned, this method alone can be**

fairly weak. For the words that you write down to reach your active vocabulary (and long term memory) you must create a review schedule for them. Otherwise, you may end up with notebooks filled with foreign words that you can't recognize after a few months, just like I initially did.

- **The Memory Palace Technique.** This was one of the earliest techniques that I encountered, when I first began to experiment with ways to learn large amounts of vocabulary quickly. The gist of it involves imagining a place (it could be based in reality like your childhood home or completely fabricated), and associating the words with a location and item in the space.
For example, if I want to learn the word "gato" (cat) in Spanish, I might picture a cat in the corner of the bedroom of my fictional house. This association with the word, location in the Memory Palace, and the image of a cat in a corner will help anchor the word "gato" into my memory.
- Personally, this method did not work very well for me. I have a vivid imagination, and often the story or the association would stick in my memory longer than the actual word that I was trying to learn. What the memory palace intends to do by providing some context to words, can be achieved with much greater effect by simply **studying in different physical places.** So instead of studying at your desk, move to the couch in the living room for a change of scenery and a boost in memory retention. When you study in different environments, positions, or scenarios you will associate that setting with any words that you encounter during the study session.

The effect will be longer lasting retention of the word and less effort exerted to conjure an image about a cat in a corner.

- **Mnemonics.** Mnemonics are very similar to the memory palace technique in the context of language learning. It seeks to use the word itself to create visual imagery, thus allowing it to root itself into memory.

For example: Let's say you wanted to learn the Spanish word "ametrelladora" (pronounced Ah-may-tray-ya-do-ra), which means machine gun. In order to use the mnemonic technique, I would break it up into its syllables and form an image based on those parts.

  - ame-tre-lla-dora - Here's my story: *ame* - looks and sound like it does in "America" so I picture the continental United States, *tre* - looks like "tree" so I picture a giant tree, *lla* - sounds like the the "ya" at the beginning of the word "yacht", now I have a yacht in my story, *dora* - Reminds me of "Dora the Explorer."

So I picture Dora, firing a machine gun at a giant tree from the back of a yacht on a lake shaped like the continental United States.

This is a pretty powerful image, and I'm likely to remember elements of it that will help me recall that "ametrelladora" means machine gun in Spanish. However, just like the memory palace, if your imagination goes too crazy, it is easy to forget why you created the image in the first place, and what you were supposed to remember about it. Keep that in mind if you decide to use this or the memory palace technique.

My Method for Learning Vocab

This is my personal method for learning new vocabulary words. I find the majority of the words that I learn within the context of what I read and listen to, which helps to anchor it into my memory. I have used this process to learn hundreds of Spanish medical terms within one month that I needed to learn for my job as an interpreter. The method is quite effective.

Of course, you can and should come up with a process that best fits your needs and your learning style. Only use mine as a guide.

- Step 1: Type/write down the unfamiliar word
- Step 2: Look up the word in a dictionary (use a monolingual dictionary if you're more advanced)
- Step 3: Look up a picture of the word online to help associate the word with a meaning
- Step 4: Search for a native pronunciation of the word online using forvo.com or a similar website
- Step 5: Create recordings of yourself saying the word for review. This final step is crucial for providing the repetition that you need for the word to reach "level 3" status and put it into your active vocabulary. It will also help me gauge how your pronunciation has improved over time.

    Step 5.1: Say the word in your native language

> *Step 5.2*: Pause for the amount of time it takes you to say the word in your mind (in your target language)
>
> *Step 5.3*: Say the word in your target language

- *Step 6*: Review the term every 2 weeks by rewriting it again, until 2 months have passed or you have completely integrated it into your long term memory, whichever comes first.

This process was labor and time intensive for me at first, but after I did it a few times it became second nature; now I spend no more than 30 minutes a day studying and reviewing vocabulary.

Learning Numbers. Although some language learners may classify numbers as just vocabulary words (which they are), I've decided to talk about them separately. Why? Because, they can be intimidating to learn for some language learners.

The good thing about learning numbers is that they tend to be highly repetitive, which makes them some of the easiest vocabulary to learn in my opinion.

Most languages have unique words for numbers 0 through 10, and may have another set of words for eleven through twenty, but after twenty, the numbers usually continue to repeat themselves in an organized pattern until you reach one-hundred. From there, it's just a matter of learning the words for the thousands, tens-of-thousands and so on.

While learning numbers may still seem frightening after that explanation, below are some techniques that you can use to learn numbers quickly and easily:

Tower of Babbling

- <u>Only count numbers in your target language wherever you see them</u>: Numbers are everywhere when you begin to notice them. They're on street signs, our phones, advertisements, literally everywhere! If you look up from this book now, it is highly likely that you can find at least one number in your field of vision without even moving from where you are. Yes it's that easy to practice numbers. Take advantage of these numbers and say them out loud whenever you see them. It will take some effort at first to drown out the numbers in your native language, but over time you will quickly memorize at least 0 through 10, then you can move on from there.
- <u>Play the license plate game</u>: This is another one of my favorites, and it is a perfect activity for a long ride in any vehicle whether you are driving or you are a passenger. Simply read the numbers on license plates as you see them on the road to practice. What makes this one so effective is that you can make the game more difficult by forcing yourself to read the plates that contain more numbers as one number.

  For example, if you see a truck with the license plate number: X638912, you could read the numbers individually as 6-3-8-9-1-2 or as two-digit numbers 63-89-12 or as triple-digit numbers 638-912, or as a single number 638,912.

  Doing this activity will allow you to practice the various numbers at the same time. I struggled with Spanish numbers until I began to play this game. After 3 months, I never had a problem with them again. It's very effective.

- <u>Do math problems</u>: I know many people have a strong dislike for math, but it is an effective way to learn numbers in your target language. The math that you do doesn't need to be college-level calculus or algebra to be effective. You can do simple addition, subtraction, multiplication, and division to get the practice.

  Math problems will force you to do calculations in your target language. The more you juggle the digits around in your head in your target language, the faster they will embed themselves in your memory.

  You can get a book with math problems or go online and find sample math problems to practice in order to do this. I recommend that you work out the solutions by hand though, because it will provide you with a kinesthetic memory element, which will further ensure that the numbers make their way into your long-term memory.

Things to Avoid: Intermediate Vocabulary

As mentioned earlier you should avoid trying to memorize long lists of vocabulary words. I understand that if you are studying a language in a formal academic setting this may be unavoidable. But on your own time, use any of the techniques in this section to learn the terms that are relevant to you and your needs.

Avoid thinking that you've learned a word after seeing it once or twice. I have made this mistake many times in the past. Schedule regular review periods or use a spaced repetition system to ensure that you are learning the words.

Finally, resist the temptation to leave your vocabulary acquisition to osmosis. Meaning, even a lousy system is better than no system at all. Even if you are studying your language in a country that speaks your target language, without deliberate practice, you will not learn the words!

Action Items for Intermediate Learners: Studying Grammar

Remember that grammar resource that you purchased in the Advanced Beginner phase? Now, it's time to pull it out and give it a closer look.

Just like vocabulary, grammar is best learned in context; however, grammar tends to be easier to deal with because every language has a fixed number of rules. After you have learned these rules, you probably won't have to ever study them intensely again for that language, unless your skills atrophy due to lack of use.

How to Solidify Your Grammar

Trying to understand when to use the subjunctive mood in Spanish and the difference between "arimasu" for inanimate objects and "imasu" for animate objects in Japanese, can be a near impossible task without enough examples to be able to tell the difference. These specific rules are easily explained in a few pages in a grammar book, but are not so easy to remember in real time speech for beginners in a language.

Now that you have more exposure to the language and a better understanding of how it should sound, it will be easier to read about the concept in a grammar book and internalize it. Below is a step-by-step process to approach absorbing grammar rules for your language.

- **Step 1**: Choose **one** grammar concept from your grammar resource.
- **Step 2**: Immediately, start practicing using that concept. Use it as many times as possible throughout the day in any situation that makes sense.
- **Step 3**: Look for usage examples of that grammar convention in context as you read, listen, or have conversations with the language. This step is key for understanding when it should be used in real life among native speakers and solidifying it in speech.

If you choose one grammar concept a day and complete this process, it is possible that you will have learned and internalized most, if not all, the grammar concepts in your language within one month. **The key is to focus on one concept at a time**, instead of trying to run through the exercises in your grammar book and expect to have learned them.

A Word on Verb Conjugation

Learning how to conjugate verbs correctly in another language can be frustrating and time consuming. If you're studying a language like Chinese that has no verb conjugations, good for you. But the reality is that most languages require some form of conjugation with their verbs, and skipping it altogether will leave you with a possible lifetime of unnatural sounding speech. For this reason, it is critical that you pay attention to verb conjugation early on in your grammar study. Below is my advice on how to deal with this often daunting aspect of learning another language:

- Tip 1: **Write it down.** Write down the root word **and** its conjugated form, any time you come across it while reading, listening, speaking, or writing. Also include the name of the form that you conjugated it to.
Example for Spanish: correr - corrió (3rd person preterit - past tense)
- Tip 2: **Look for patterns.** Most languages have a fixed system for conjugating their verbs. Like the Spanish "ar" "er" and "ir" verbs, they all conjugate in the same way within their respective categories. These patterns generally repeat themselves and once you've learned them they will become automatic. Of course, there will be exceptions to the rules that you will have to learn separately, but with the basic patterns memorized, you will be able to conjugate a large number of words easily.
- Tip 3: **Use flashcards or SRS flashcards.** Any words that you write down to focus on conjugation, consider studying them as if they were a completely new word. For example, you could make a flashcard for the word "食べる" (taberu), which means 'to eat' in Japanese, and make a separate card for "食べらなかった" (taberanakatta) which means 'did not eat' to show the conjugation for the past tense dictionary form. Do the same for any other conjugation that you want to learn.
- Tip 4: **Do not try to learn all of the conjugated forms all at once.** I remember in my high school French class, going over all of the conjugated forms

of one verb in the conjugation tables of the textbook. The result was that I learned only two of the forms well (the ones I needed to pass the class) and forgot the others. It can be tempting to do this when you study on your own, because many online resources will show a conjugation table of the various forms of almost **every** verb in that language. **Trust me, you will not remember all of these forms, and it is a waste of time and effort to try and learn this way.**

Finding the words in their conjugated form in context is the best way to learn how and when to use that form. After you encounter that verb conjugation enough times, you will begin to internalize the structure and eventually it will become second nature for you to recognize it in oral and written form and to produce it during a conversation.

Things to Avoid: Intermediate Grammar

Drilling grammar concepts without other forms of practice. Drilling grammar (using exercises in textbooks, online, etc.) is not bad in and of itself. But the grammar is less likely to stick if all you do is complete the exercises and move on to the next grammar concept. After all that's probably what you had to do in school and it probably wasn't a very effective way to learn it.

You need repeated examples of grammar in spoken and written context. You also need to practice using it when you speak to reinforce the grammar drills. Drills are great for reviewing concepts, but not very effective alone, especially when you are being exposed to a concept for the first time.

Not adapting grammar knowledge to real life speech. Textbooks will often describe grammar in one way, but native speakers may use it differently or not at all in casual speech. This is just like in American English. A grammatically correct way to express a future action that someone will take is "going to do". However, many people will use the more casual and easier to say "gonna do", which omits the preposition "to" and completely changes the gerund form of the verb "go". You probably won't find "gonna" on an official English verb conjugation table, despite its regular use among millions of native English speakers in the U.S. and abroad.

You must adapt your speech to the way native speakers actually speak sometimes if you want to be understood, and learn to recognize when native speakers break or ignore rules in their own language.

Not studying grammar at all. As a student it is essential that you refine your grammar usage at this level to ensure the accuracy of your speech and pronunciation. It also ensures that you haven't developed any bad habits in your speech from learning from friends or TV shows.

Action Items for Intermediate Learners: Intermediate Reading

At this level you should begin to consume more materials that primarily feature your target language. For that reason, anything with translations readily available in your native and target language will be helpful.

I've found that at the intermediate level, it is often most difficult to find materials because you are not a beginner anymore, yet native level materials are still out of reach. Below are my suggestions for some resources that will be beneficial for improving reading at this level:

- Elementary School Readers
- Children's/Young Adult Stories
- Comic books

These are just a few examples of good sources of intermediate materials; of course there are others that work just as well. The main characteristic that the materials should have at this level is that they should contain fairly simple vocabulary and grammatical structures. They should also primarily feature your target language.

Things to Avoid: Intermediate Reading

Trying to read materials that are too advanced. Take your time and be patient with reading easier materials like those listed above when you start. After you feel more comfortable reading and you can produce the language somewhat smoothly, you should move on to more difficult resources.

Not reading out loud. Whenever you don't read out loud, you are missing out on a valuable opportunity to improve your fluency. I know it can feel awkward to do this, but if you make it a habit early on it will stay with you throughout the rest of your studies.

Action Items for Intermediate Learners: Intermediate Speaking

At this point, you will probably have the ability to have basic conversations in your target language. For this reason, this is a good time to introduce a regular conversation partner into your practice routine.

Conversation Partners

The criteria for a good conversation partner is very similar to finding a good tutor, which you can review in *Chapter 3 (Advanced Beginner: Consider Getting A Tutor)*.

The only difference is to ensure that the person you choose to practice with is not too far below or above your level. This can be difficult to gauge, but you will be able to tell if the fit is appropriate if you feel like you are having a somewhat natural conversation in your target language.

If the partner is too far **below** your level, you won't get the practice you need and you will essentially become their tutor.

If the partner is too far **above** your level, it will most likely transform into a mostly one-sided conversation, leaving you with little opportunity to practice as you constantly try to figure out what they're saying. Be careful to avoid both extremes.

Taking and Receiving Feedback

Consider speaking with a tutor, friend, relative, etc. and ask for honest feedback. Feedback is critical at this phase, because even though your fluency is improving, it is still very possible to develop bad habits with pronunciation, grammar, and language usage. This happens sometimes when we spend too much time practicing speaking on our own and can't hear our own mistakes. Find someone you trust and **ask** for feedback. Sometimes that is the only way to get it.

Don't be afraid to go solo

If you don't have access to any of the above, you can still get speaking practice. You will have to look for ANY opportunity to use the language even if it feels out of place or stupid. This may include talking to yourself by describing your daily activities or speaking to people around you who don't speak your language. It may feel uncomfortable at first, but you will still be getting valuable practice with the language.

When it comes to receiving feedback, you will have to do it for yourself, which can be tricky. The best way to get better at finding your own mistakes, is by increasing the amount of listening that you do and learning the grammar of the language. This way you will know how the language should sound and can begin to hold yourself to that standard when you speak.

You can also record yourself while you read and play it back to review your renditions. Were you using the the right rhythm, tone, and pronunciation? How was your accent? Evaluating yourself may not seem as effective as having outside feedback, but it does work. It can also save you time and potentially money, since you will not have to pay anyone or wait for them to be available to receive feedback.

Things to Avoid: Intermediate Speaking

Thinking that you are fluent because you can say a few things very well. After your first few successful conversations in your language, it can be tempting to believe that you don't need to practice as much anymore. This couldn't be farther from the truth.

At this point, you still need regular speaking practice to be able to use the language spontaneously and naturally, so that you can solidify your skills in your mind.

Not using the language enough: being afraid of making mistakes. I mentioned this pitfall briefly in the Chapter 2, but it is even more important to avoid it as an Intermediate speaker. Now that you have been exposed to more of the language, you will realize more of the things that you don't know about it. As a result, some of us begin to focus more on the aspects of the language that we don't know or are weak in, than we do on the aspects of the language that we have perfected.

This mentality can be crippling to your progress. It's important that even though you are more aware of the mistakes that you make while speaking, you continue to push through the discomfort and improve your skills.

Action Items for Intermediate Learners: Intermediate Listening

As your speaking improves, it is equally important to increase your listening skills along with it. After all, it's difficult to have a conversation if you can't understand what the other person is saying. Listening to audio sources with more natural dialogue, rather than slower and beginner ones will help you train your ear for the **real** language that native speakers use. Here are some suggestions for focusing on your listening skills:

Listening to native speaker content materials at slower speeds. Many audio and video players allow you to listen to recordings at slower speeds. This could be a good way to get started with sounds and grammar patterns that are difficult to understand when you first begin to listen to materials recorded with native speech.

CAUTION Be careful with spending too much time listening to materials at slower speeds. Eventually, you want to be able to understand people speaking the language at natural speed. If you spend too much time listening to slower speech, your brain may adapt to it, and you will still struggle to understand native speakers. Consider using it briefly to fine tune your skills, but transition to speech spoken at normal speed as soon as possible.

Watch easy materials that you are already familiar with in your target language (with subtitles). A great source of listening materials are older TV shows, movies, and cartoons that have been dubbed into your target language. Since you have already watched them in the past, you will already be familiar with the characters and the story, which will allow you to focus more on the language. Early on during my Spanish studies, I watched old episodes of Pokémon dubbed into Spanish with English subtitles. That helped me grasp the basics of the language, with relatively simple speech spoken by native speakers.

A Thought on the Use of Subtitles When you first begin to watch dubbed materials, you will probably naturally want to have the subtitles on so that you can understand what the characters are saying. While this is helpful for comprehension, it is not the best way to improve your **listening** ability, because you will be **reading** the subtitles as you watch.

Consider watching the material at least twice, **once with subtitles on and a second time with the subtitles off.** This way during the second watch, you will be able to understand the context of what's being said and can focus on the actual speech that is being used.

Find materials with more realistic dialogue (not dialogue meant for language learners). It can be difficult to bridge the gap between the spoken audio found in many language courses, and actual language that you will hear in regular conversation with native or fluent speakers, but it is an important step.

Depending on which language tool you chose during your Beginner and Advanced Beginner phase, you may or may not have been training with realistic audio up to this point. This will definitely be to your advantage, since you won't have to make a large adjustment in your training to account for normal speech.

If you are beginning self-study after having recently completed formal academic classes in your language, you should be more aware of this potential pitfall. Language classes at the high school and college level tend work with dialogues that, while effective at teaching you the correct usage of the language, would sound unnatural to hear in casual conversations with native speakers. You will have to compensate for this by actively using materials that will give you a better idea of what everyday conversations really sound like.

A Thought On Clean Vs. Raw Audio Often when we begin to learn a language we use sources of audio that are "clean." In this context, clean audio means audio that is produced to sound as clear and understandable as possible. Audio in radio broadcasts, podcasts, and many language learning materials often contain audio that has passed through expensive microphones and sophisticated sound equipment. This audio is fantastic when you begin to learn a language because you will be able to hear nuances of speech much more clearly than you would in raw unfiltered audio.

As you know, most conversations in real life are raw. There's always something like the noise of traffic, a blaring TV, or other ambient noises that can make understanding what the other person is trying to say difficult. If you want to be prepared to understand the the language anywhere and in any context, I recommend that you really begin to focus on resources that contain raw audio as an intermediate learner.

A good place to start is with the local news online or on the radio. News broadcasts have studio sections with high quality audio (clean audio) and interviews that often take place outside or in noisy office environments (raw audio). This way you will receive a good balance of both forms of audio. You can focus on acquiring new vocabulary with the clean audio and get used to hearing it when there are noises that distract from the language itself during the raw audio segments.

Things to Avoid: Intermediate Listening

Passive listening (doesn't work). It can be tempting to turn on some audio and just let it play in the background while you do something else like wash the dishes or clean up around the house to get listening practice. I can tell you from personal experience that this does not work when you still have to work to understand the audio as a low-intermediate learner. You may feel like you're making progress, but in reality your brain is filtering out most of what you are hearing as noise.

Unless you can understand at least 70% of what you are listening to, having the audio of your target language on while you do other activities **will not** improve your listening skills at this level! Take the time to actively listen to the material, or find simpler audio to work with.

Using movies/series/TV shows (that you are not familiar with) as tools too soon. After you have gotten used to watching older TV shows and movies, you will be burning to try out authentic media in your target language. I encourage you to avoid diving into media content created for native audiences at this point.

If you've made it this far with your studies in your target language, you probably really enjoy some aspects of the culture, and as a result you will want to absorb every detail possible in the materials that you watch. The foreign locations, the unfamiliar customs and food, the story, are all things that will catch your attention, and at this point it will be too overwhelming to absorb it all. You may be able to understand some of what you hear at this point, but it won't be enough for you to get much out of the materials. Other problems include:

- Getting distracted by the action/story and not focusing on the language
- Being confused by heavy use of slang and idioms which make comprehension difficult
- Being frustrated by confusing accents, dialogue spoken at a low volume, etc. and other distractions that make comprehension difficult

Avoid these materials for now (unless you can understand at least 70% of what you hear). Come back later when you can get more out of the materials than just disparate words and phrases every few minutes.

Having too much comfort with studying beginner materials. As I have mentioned before, the language learning market is saturated with materials available on and off-line. Once you've found a study resource that you like in the early phases of your studying, it can be tempting to keep using it as you advance. After all, you're used to the speaker's style and voice, and it took you weeks to find that perfect podcast or app that wasn't too fast but still challenged you. I know this feeling well.

In a way, it is great that you've found a resource that contains enough challenging materials that were able to take you from being language curious to an intermediate level in a language. That's pretty rare. However, an overreliance on one learning tool limits your growth. You need to become used to various styles of speech, vocabulary, accents, dialects, and idioms in your materials. This is especially true if you are studying on your own

outside of an area where the language is commonly spoken. You will not receive variety in the language through mere exposure, like a student who can walk outside and hear hundreds of examples of people using the language in numerous different ways.

As an independent language learner, you have to be proactive in exposing yourself to different sides of the language. For example, there will be no one to tell you when to begin to pay attention to slang or casual speech, as opposed to the more formal and polite speech that tends to be front loaded in most language learning tools.

Therefore, only you can know for sure when it's time to move on and find more challenging materials. But I would say if you have been using the same resource for at least **3 months and it doesn't scare you a little to turn it on to improve in the language,** you should begin to look actively look for materials that use more complex language and that possibly cover an aspect of the language and culture that you're unfamiliar with. You've probably mastered any materials that you used in the first two levels at this point anyway and are not getting as much out of them as you were previously when you had less experience with the language.

Put them aside and challenge yourself with more difficult tools. This is the only way that you'll continue improving.

Materials created by non-native speakers. Spoken materials created by non-native speakers can be a mixed bag. On one hand, they can be beneficial because they will often have a good balance between material in the source and target language, and they can definitely relate to your struggles with learning the language.

However, some have questionable language skills, and on top of that, they most likely will not have a native accent, which is what you need to be listening to at this level.

I know that it is highly possible for a non-native speaker to reach a level of fluency that you cannot tell the difference between them and a native speaker. While that may be the case, you must be selective in the materials that you choose to listen to. Literally anybody can start their own blog, podcast, or YouTube channel and teach a language, and that instruction may not be of the highest quality.

Therefore, you should stick with materials that contain native speaker audio just to be on the safe side. If you can't tell whether the voice is of a native speaker or not, then that's a good sign that it's probably safe to use that audio source for listening content. If not, put it aside until your listening skills have improved or find audio created by native speakers.

Action Items for Intermediate Learners: Intermediate Writing

Few people deliberately practice writing in a foreign language. It is often a skill that is regarded as "nice to have" but not necessary for true proficiency in the language. Before you skip this section entirely, you must realize that if you ever plan to be able to use your language skills in a professional capacity, you will need some writing skills to be able qualify for many positions. Furthermore, writing practice will help you quickly realize your weaknesses with the grammar of the language, which is another reason why it is important to develop at least basic writing skills.

When many people think of writing, they think of writing long pieces like essays and books, but you don't have to go to such extremes to practice. Here are some simple ideas that will help you take small steps to practice writing in your target language:

Text your friends. **Texting is an easy way to practice writing short basic phrases in your target language. This works better if you have friends who speak your target language, but you can also try it with friends who only speak your native language too. Just tell them to keep a translation app or website on hand and they should be fine. Who knows, maybe you will convince them to try learning your target language as well!**

CAUTION While texting is a great place to begin with writing practice, you want to avoid developing the habit of using shorthand messages that are common when texting in actual written correspondence in a professional setting. This especially true when texting native speakers, who will often use shorthand and slang that is common among casual acquaintances, but has no place in a workplace exchange.

Take notes. This is another easy place to start practicing writing. Need to make a grocery list for the store or take notes during a session with your tutor or your conversation partner? **Consider writing in your target language.** You probably won't have to use full sentences, so like texting it's a great way to see how it feels to write in the language.

A good way to form the habit of writing, is to challenge yourself to write in your chosen language whenever you are doing things related to studying the language. You could try setting up your next tutoring session in your target language or practice by writing down any new words that you want to learn next time you do listening practice. Be creative with how you slowly introduce writing into your language learning and it will quickly go from challenging and awkward, to being second nature.

Keep a journal. If you don't have anyone who you would want to text or if you'd rather work on your own, consider keeping a journal in your target language. This is a great way to not only practice your writing, but to record your progress with the language as well. Don't worry if the sentences are basic and simple, just the act of writing will help you begin to form and structure sentences in your head organically, which is exactly what you will have to do to become fluent in speaking the language.

For those of you at a loss for words, here are some ideas for journal writing prompts that you can use:

- Journal about studying your language
- Describe your study space
- Write about what you did during the day
- A reaction to new materials that you used to study the language
- Rewrite your reasons why you decided to study the language and evaluate your progress
- Talk about a future trip you would like to take to a country that speaks your language

There are tons more potential journal topics online. It doesn't matter what you write about, it only matters that you practice forming your own sentences, and reading them back to see how well you used the conventions of the language.

I personally did this during the first year that I was studying Spanish and it really improved my grammar and my vocabulary. I used to set a timer on my phone for 20 to 30 minutes and write as much as I could until my alarm went off. Usually that was enough time to get at least 10 sentences on the screen/paper.

A note on writing by hand vs. typing Some of you may be asking yourself with respect to writing: "Should I learn how to write the language by hand? Or should I just practice typing on my computer and texting on my digital device?" The answer to this question depends on your individual needs and goals with the target language.

Some language learning purists will tell you that by learning to write language scripts like Chinese or Japanese by hand, you will be capturing the essence and spirit of the language and you can learn it more easily this way. While that may be somewhat true, I'm not so sentimental when it comes to this.

The reality is that our need to be able to write by hand in our **native languages,** has been reduced significantly since computers became mainstream in the early 2000s. When was the last time you wrote a letter or anything official by hand since you finished your formal education? When was the last time you **had** to do it? Probably not recently.

If this same trend is applied to your target language, then you will find that you have even less of a need to produce any writing by hand.

With that said, I understand that there may be specific occupational cases which **require** you to write the language down by hand. Here are a few examples:

Intermediate Level

- Needing to able to take rapid notes in a foreign language, because it will be more convenient for a recipient who speaks it to read later on
- Needing to be able to produce written script by hand because you are working with a language that has little or no access to digital technology
- Needing to write the language because you are researching a language with few written records, and you are trying to document the language

There are of course other scenarios which would necessitate knowing how to write a language by hand. However, for most independent language learners, learning to write the language by hand is probably outside of the scope of their language goals.

The bottom line is, since you will most likely be using some piece of digital technology to produce any type of written message in your target language, it is best to focus on learning to produce the language through the various digital applications available for your respective language. If you feel inclined to learn how to produce a script like Japanese Kanji by hand just for fun, then by all means do so. But know that the chances of it serving a practical purpose are slim to none.

Things to Avoid: Intermediate Writing

Not practicing writing at all. Even as someone who generally enjoys writing, I struggled to practice it early on in my Spanish studies. It will be difficult at first, but know that your effort will be beneficial at some point in the future if you keep it up.

Also, don't forget that all modalities are linked. Being a stronger writer, will make you a better speaker. Strong reading skills will make you a better writer and so on. So pairing a writing block after a reading or speaking block is a great way reinforce your abilities in multiple areas.

Sample Study Plan for Intermediate Learners

As in the advanced beginner phase, it will be helpful for you to break up your studies into two days. This will help you better focus on the tasks that you set out to complete for that day. This schedule is programmed to include all modalities in a language, but it can and should be modified to fit your unique goals.

Two day schedule (alternate days)

Day 1

- **Vocab Study/Review.** Review any words encountered on the previous day(s) (The amount of words will depend of on your language goals): **15%**
- **Grammar.** Review at least one grammar concept and use it throughout the day: **15%**
- **Reading. 35%**
- **Listening.** (Can be through a conversation partner or by listening to short audios): **35%**

Day 2

- **Vocab Study/Review.** Review any words encountered on the previous day(s): **15%**
- **Grammar.** Review at least one grammar concept and use it throughout the day: **15%**
- **Speaking.** (Can be with a tutor or through reading): **35%**
- **Writing. 35%**

A Few Cautions Regarding the Intermediate Study Schedule

Trying to do too many things in one day - You know you are at an Intermediate level with a language when you realize how much you **don't** know in the language. A typical response to this realization is to try learning everything at once, which is impossible and discouraging. Do what you can with the time you have available, but be sure to allow your mind to absorb all of the information that you have fed it during your study by taking a rest after an intense session. This will make it easier for you to re-engage the next day.

Not focusing on your desired modality - With so many aspects of the language that you want to improve it can be a challenge to focus on one area at a time. A listening session can quickly transform into a grammar session, and a grammar session can transform to focus on vocabulary if you don't keep your objective in focus.

Of course all of the modalities overlap, but by being distracted from the primary goal of your activity, you will slow down your progress with all of them, not to mention waste precious time. Remember, focusing on one modality at a time will give you the best results in the long run.

Wanting to look up/know EVERY word - This was and still is probably one of my biggest issues with learning languages. Have you ever come across a ten word sentence, couldn't understand five of the words, and stopped to look them all up in a dictionary? I used to do this all the time and it literally added months to my acquisition of Spanish. Worst of all, because I had no reliable system to learn vocabulary in place at the time, I had no way to get these words into my long term memory. Basically, after I looked them up, they were usually gone and forgotten by the end of the day.

I know how frustrating it can be to read a news article for an hour and not be able to really understand the full context of what you just read. However, stopping to look up **every** unknown word was part of the problem. It pulled me away from what I was reading so much that I couldn't get as much out of my reading practice. Don't let this happen to you.

If you establish a reliable method for learning new vocabulary (See *Create a Plan for Building Your Vocabulary*), you will eventually learn more than enough new vocabulary terms as you encounter them during any portion of your studies. It takes patience, but you will get there.

Being too hard on yourself. This advice is so important that I've had to include it nearly all of the "Things to avoid" sections. Yes, it's that important! Why? Because it is something that most if not all language learners deal with at some point or another. We wonder why we can't manage to pronounce certain words correctly even though we've heard them hundreds of times. Or why we still get nervous when speaking to a native speaker, always thinking about if or when they will ask us a question that we can't understand or don't know how to respond to. These are fears that haunt us all, even after we've achieved a decent level of fluency.

The fact is that if you made it this far in your studies and contemplated giving up trying to reach your language goals, you are definitely not alone. You **will** struggle during this phase, but it is completely normal. By now, your close friends and family know that you are learning this language, and it can feel embarrassing not to be able to speak fluently or understand the language completely. Don't worry about that. Know that you are making progress at your own pace and believe that your effort and dedication will result in you achieving the language goals that you've set for yourself. **Don't give up!**

Estimated Length Of Time At The Intermediate Level?

Approximately 8 months - 15 months

I know that this may seem like a long time amount to reach fluency and it surely can feel that way, especially if you are working at your language every day in some way. One of the factors that often causes this time to drag on even longer than the estimated 15 months is our level of motivation or lack thereof.

When we begin studying a new language, especially as an independent learner, we tend to dive in headfirst with enthusiasm to begin learning and speaking the language. Unfortunately, as time goes on and we advance to the mid- to upper- intermediate level, we realize how much further we have to go and how much more time and effort that we will have to commit to reach our goals, and our commitment falters as a result.

Suddenly, we begin to justify not putting in our dedicated study time, making excuses not to study, and as a result our hard earned progress begins to backslide as we become lost in the process, unsure of our next move. We become stranded on a plateau of uncertainty, not sure if we even want to continue with the language at all.

For me personally, I spent a little over 12 months on the intermediate plateau with Spanish, and during that time I experienced all of the aforementioned emotions outlined above. We'll talk in more detail about the language plateau that tends to greet all students sometime around the mid- and upper-intermediate level, as well as some strategies to get off of and avoid it completely at the end of this chapter.

I consider the intermediate level to be the true test of not only how strong your determination is to learn the language in a way that meets your goals, but also the strength of the process that you have constructed to reach that goal.

Many independent learners set out with determination and no plan. But without a basic plan of how to succeed, their determination flags and their progress slows to a crawl.

This book will help you form your plan, your job is to stay motivated to work a little bit everyday, so that you meet your goals in a reasonable amount of time.

How to Know When to Move On To the Next Level

With so many aspects of the language that you have improved on, it can be difficult to accurately assess yourself and know that you are ready to move on to the advanced level. As I mentioned in the advanced beginner chapter, your ability to be as honest with yourself as possible will help you decide whether or not you are prepared to

Intermediate Level

promote yourself. Use the following tests to assess your progress:

Go back to materials that you used for **listening** practice when you began the **intermediate** level and ask yourself:

- How does this sound to me?
- Does it sound slow?
- Does the vocabulary sound very simple? Can I follow the speaker easily?
- If you can answer these questions positively, you might be ready to move on.

Go back to materials that you used for **reading** practice when you began the **intermediate** level and ask yourself:

- Do I recognize the majority of the sentence constructions (grammar)?
- Can I read the material in my target language fairly easily without consulting a dictionary often?
- Can I understand most of the message of what I'm reading as opposed to just individual sentences and words?
- If you can answer these questions positively, you might be ready to move on.

Consult a tutor/friend/family member and ask them how your **speaking** has improved since you began studying the language. This will be highly subjective, but it may give you an indication of how well you've improved since you started learning.

Try shadowing - If you are studying on your own, **shadowing** is a great way to gauge your speaking ability and improve fluency. Shadowing involves repeating exactly what you hear on any recording by following the tone, intonation, and rhythm of the recording as closely as possible, staying just a second or two behind the actual recording.

To evaluate your speaking ability, try shadowing materials that you have listened to or read earlier in your studies and ask yourself the following questions:

You can measure your **writing** capabilities by giving yourself a random writing prompt to see how well you can communicate basic thoughts in your own words. If what you wrote makes sense, you might be ready to move on.

Reassess your Language Confidence Level (LCL). If it is at least a **25/35,** you are probably ready to move on. (*Refer to Getting Started: Chapter 1 for an explanation of the LCL*)

General Notes on the Intermediate Level

I can say from personal experience that this is the most difficult level of the language learning process. You will be floating in between knowing enough for basic communication, but not knowing enough to express yourself fully or understand when others express themselves, for period of time that can last for months or years. Also, the general lack of learning materials at this stage can harm your progress, especially if you are learning a language that is less widely spoken.

All of these factors often lead students to reach a plateau in their language development, which can sometimes even make them quit. If you do plateau, once again realize that this is normal.

Successfully navigating and eventually exiting the plateau can take significant effort, but it is possible and necessary if you plan to ever reach your language goals.

On the Plateau

The first step to moving past the plateau is to realize that you are on it. Here are some of the signs that you have reached a stagnation point with your language learning process and that it might be time for a change:

- You're bored when you study and don't look forward to it anymore
- You make excuses for not using the language
- You can't focus on the language anymore and you are tempted to start learning another language or something else entirely
- You "took a break" from studying the language regularly, and feel too far behind to start up again
- You lie to yourself and tell yourself that you are "already fluent" even though you know it is just memorized fluency
- You have no idea what you should do to continue studying the language
- You had a consistent study plan, but stopped following it and are not motivated to start it again
- You feel like you are not making progress with any aspect of the language
- You keep making the same mistakes when you try to use the language in a conversation
- You feel like you are becoming worse with the language despite continued practice

- You've considered quitting the language completely because your goal seems impossible to reach

These are classic signs that a cold wind is blowing atop the plateau, and that you need to change some things about how you engage with the language. The changes can be subtle or they can be drastic, but something needs to happen quickly before you drop the language and your goals entirely.

Getting off of the plateau

The following are some suggestions for how to get off of the plateau and breathe new life into your language studies.

Evaluate what's not working. Look carefully at the materials and resources that you have been using to practice the language. Maybe you found an outstanding podcast that you liked, but you've listened to all of the episodes multiple times. Or perhaps, you've had the same conversation partner for months, and now that you're used to their style, you're not growing anymore.

Only by knowing what materials are dragging you down, can you begin to work to revitalize your interest in the language.

Replace what's not working. Consider replacing elements of your training with new ones that you are unfamiliar with. Watch a series with a different dialect of the language, instead of going to the same restaurant or club to practice the language, try a place you've never been to across town. These changes may be inconvenient at first, but you will force yourself back into growth mode when you do them.

Intermediate Level

Take a trip. Put your language skills to the test by going to a place where it is the lingua franca. You may not be completely fluent or understand everything that you read or hear, but doing this before you feel like you are ready can give you a huge confidence boost and revive your interest in the language. You might just surprise yourself at how well you do!

Challenge yourself. Mini challenges are a good way to see how far you've come and improve your skill at the same time. You can challenge yourself for a week, a month, or longer. The point is to change up your tired study routine and bring the language to life in a more dynamic way. The following are some suggestions of challenges that you can do:

- Only read news in your target language
- Challenge yourself to only speak your language during the day
- Only write short notes in your language
- Listen to or watch a video and summarize it (in your native or target language) for a friend, partner, tutor, or parent
- Speak about random topics using **only** your target language

There are tons of other examples of language challenges that you can find online. Look a few up and try them!

You can also include your friends and family in your challenges to make it more fun and to help hold you accountable for them. You will find that challenges are excellent ways to use the language in creative ways that will stretch your current abilities in a fun and memorable way.

Remind yourself of your language goals. You started learning this language for a reason, and the middle of a plateau is a great time to remind yourself what that reason was. Think of all of the people that you have met through your studies and how far you have come up to this point. Several months ago you could barely form one coherent sentence and now you can probably have at least a basic conversation with the language. That's a huge accomplishment!

How many people have you known who talked about learning a language yet never took any action to do it? Probably several. Unlike them, you have taken significant steps to reach your goal (mostly on your own) and you should be proud of that.

Set up an immersion environment

It can be intimidating to set up an immersion environment for the first time. Initially, there will be many things that you don't understand that will possibly impede your ability to get things done. On the other hand, it is a great way to force yourself to pay attention to different aspects of the language that you may have overlooked during your previous studies. If you feel like you are ready for it, an immersion environment will help you push your language ability to the next level. Here are some ways that you can do it:

- Label objects in your house with sticky notes that contain translations or short sentences

- Change the settings of any devices/apps/programs that you use to the target language
- Find a radio station in your target language and listen to it while you drive or take public transportation
- Watch TV shows or series in your target language only (or at least with subtitles in them)

These are just a few ways that you can create an immersion environment in your target language. With the amount of digital technology available, it is easy to surround yourself with your target language. You just have to be willing to take that leap to make the adjustments and instantly you will be forced to pay more attention to how you study the language.

Final thoughts on the plateau

It is possible that you will encounter multiple plateaus as you move toward your language goals. Remember, a plateau usually comes after you have worked with the same materials or content for an extended amount of time. By regularly incorporating a healthy amount of variety in your studies you can avoid them altogether.

Finally, as you become more literate in the language, you will begin to be able to make use of more content designed and produced for native speakers, which will give you as much novelty as you have in your native tongue, making plateaus in your target language forever a thing of the the past. When you've reached a point where you can pick up almost any resource and use it for study, congratulations, you know you are probably ready for the advanced level.

Intermediate Level Quick Notes

DO (VOCABULARY)
- Create a plan for building your vocabulary

DON'T (VOCABULARY)
- Memorize long lists of vocabulary words
- Think that you've learned a word after you've seen it only once or twice
- Try to learn vocabulary through osmosis

DO (GRAMMAR)
- Study or practice one grammar concept at a time
- Pay attention to verb conjugations (you will learn them intuitively through repetition and practice)

DON'T (GRAMMAR)
- Drill grammar concepts without practicing them in other ways
- Forget to adapt your grammar to the ways in which native speakers really speak
- Neglect to study grammar

DO (READING)
- Read more materials that primarily contain your target language

DON'T (READING)
- Read materials that are too advanced
- Forget to read out loud whenever possible

Intermediate Level

DO (SPEAKING)

- Find a good conversation partner
- Receive as much feedback as possible
- Speak to yourself if you have to in order to get practice

DON'T (SPEAKING)

- Think that you are fluent because you can say a few expressions very well (memorized fluency)
- Be afraid to make mistakes and not use the language because of it

DO (LISTENING)

- Listen to native speaker content at slower speeds
- Watch easy materials that you are already familiar with in your target language
- Find material with more realistic dialogue

DON'T (LISTENING)

- Use passive listening
- Watch movies/series/TV shows (that you are not familiar with) as tools too soon
- Get too comfortable with studying beginner materials
- Use materials created by non-native speakers

DO (WRITING)

- Practice using the following methods:
- Texting
- Writing notes
- Keeping a journal

DON'T (WRITING)

- Worry about learning to write by hand (unless you need or want to)
- Neglect writing completely

DO (STUDY SCHEDULE)

- Divide your schedule into a two-day alternating schedule

DON'T (STUDY SCHEDULE)

- Try to study too many things in one day
- Try to study more than one modality at a time
- Look up EVERY word in a dictionary all the time
- Be too hard on yourself

DO (THE PLATEAU)
- Recognize that you are on the plateau
- Evaluate and replace the aspects of your study that aren't working for you anymore
- Introduce more variety into your language studies by:
- Taking a trip
- Challenging yourself in a new way
- Reminding yourself of your language goals
- Setting up an immersion environment

DON'T (THE PLATEAU)
- Give up!
- Feel bad for plateauing (it happens to any serious language learner)

Advanced Level (Chapter 5)

As you walk into the sushi restaurant illuminated by the giant glowing sign "弦" (pronounced 'gen' meaning 'string of an instrument' in Japanese) on the outside you know it's going to be long night. Your business for Japanese course has gone well for the last year, and you hardly think about the mechanics of the language at all anymore, it just seems to flow, especially after you've had a few Orion beers or have a karaoke microphone thrust into your hand by your colleagues.

The night plays out as many have in the past. You talk a little business using your arsenal of Japanese, which includes some well-rehearsed phrases and expressions, but by the end of the night you realize that you've been able to get by and even produce some organic speech. You've even picked up a new word or two in the haze of cigarette smoke in the restaurant. There are still some colloquialisms and local slang that you don't quite understand when your Japanese business partners use them in normal conversation, but you plan on asking them what they mean during the next after hours meeting.

It is at that moment that it occurs to you that you've come quite a long way since deciding to take this job in Japan over a year and a half ago, and that your knowledge of Japanese is quite advanced.

Who is an Advanced Learner?

Someone who is comfortable orally expressing **most** ideas in a spontaneous manner.

A person who can **read** a large amount of materials in the **target language.**

Someone who **actively** becomes familiar with the **culture** associated with the target language.

An individual who consumes and largely understands **media** (movies, videos, books, music etc.) in the target language.

A Word of Congratulations

At this point in your studies, you are most likely fluent (even though you may not feel like it) in your language, just like the unnamed person in the short story at the beginning of this chapter. You can probably understand a wide variety of materials and people in it and communicate many things with relative ease. This is a significant achievement!

While you may have other goals associated with the language, being able to communicate freely is typically one of the goals that most people who study a foreign language have, and I know how good it feels to reach that important milestone.

Additionally, as an advanced student of the language, you now have the opportunity to take advantage of more complicated and specialized materials and to push yourself to an even higher level of professional literacy level in it. This chapter will give you some pointers on how to go farther than you ever thought you could with your language.

Action Items for Advanced Learners: Advanced Vocabulary

Continue Building Your Vocabulary!

You should never stop building your vocabulary. It is the foundation that your language ability was built on, and every new word or idiom that you acquire gives you more options for expressing yourself or understanding someone else in a more accurate manner.

Furthermore, now that your vocabulary is quite large it will be much easier to learn new words, since you simply won't encounter as many that you don't know when you use the language. New words will easily stand out when you read or hear the language. It's pretty amazing!

Keep your vocabulary system in place, but know that you won't need to rely on it as much as you did before.

Transition to using a reliable monolingual dictionary in your target language. It is a good idea at this point to transition to a monolingual dictionary in your target language, if you can find one.

The advantage of using a monolingual dictionary is that not only will you reinforce common words that you already know, but you will also learn synonyms faster and learn the definitions of words from the perspective of its culture, as opposed to learning them through translations.

Additionally, many online dictionaries contain example sentences, synonyms, antonyms, idioms and other features that will help you learn more than just the definition of the words. These extra features are fantastic resources for learning the nuances of how native speakers use the term in natural conversation and how you should be using them as well.

Initially, it may feel overwhelming to use a monolingual dictionary, because it will take longer to find and learn the definitions of certain words. But if you commit to it, after a few weeks, you will find that you will never want to go back to a standard bilingual dictionary, just because you will be extracting more of the language every time you look up a word.

There are several different options for monolingual dictionaries, especially in more commonly spoken languages, **so choose one and stick with it.** This will allow you to get used to the way entries are organized, and what additional features it may have, both of which will allow you to spend less time in the dictionary, and more time consuming content in your target language.

Advanced Level

Things to Avoid: Advanced Vocabulary

Not continuing to build your vocabulary. Many people believe that once they are fluent in a language and can understand it very well, their work with vocabulary is over. No more flashcards forever. This is a poisonous mentality to adopt when becoming literate in a foreign language.

Remember, as a non-native speaker, your chances of encountering new vocabulary are generally low unless you look for them in books, websites, TV series and other mediums. Even if you live in a country where the language is spoken regularly, you won't learn new words that you hear unless you take the time to practice them in order to incorporate them into your active vocabulary, just like you've done with all of the words you've learned up to this point. Avoid becoming complacent in your growth and continue to absorb as many new words as you can.

Action Items for Advanced Learners: Advanced Reading

Now that you can read almost anything that you want in your target language, you can focus on the cultural perspective of the materials that you read, and learning more specialized terminology rather than reading for understanding or for learning the mechanics of the language. I will discuss learning culture in more detail later in this chapter, but for now below are some suggestions for further increasing your reading skills.

Read the news

Reading the news is a great way to diversify your vocabulary and to stay informed about current events. It may be difficult at first to understand some of the more formal language used in the articles, but after you've learned the terminology, you will have access to a multifaceted tool for improving your skills.

One of the things that I like most about reading the news in another language is the sometimes dramatic shift in perspective that it offers for certain events. You will truly be seeing from the perspective of that culture's values and beliefs as opposed to the somewhat detached version often presented in translated news sources.

Finding and committing to news sources can be difficult, because there are many options to choose from. **I recommend choosing two sources, one from a larger media outlet and one from a smaller, perhaps local, source.** Both sources should provide you with enough content to broaden your perspective on a myriad of issues, while simultaneously broadening your view of the world.

Read books

Reading books is by far one of the best ways to improve and maintain your language. What makes whole books—whether they are fiction or non-fiction—stand out among other reading sources is that they can be used to improve every aspect of your language ability.

Your reading will obviously improve, along with your grammar because you will be absorbing content in context

Advanced Level

that has be proofread and edited to be as clear as possible. You can also transform books into highly effective speaking practice by reading out loud, as I have mentioned numerous times already. By doing this you will be practicing listening by hearing yourself speak, which will give you more confidence to mimic those structures in real conversations.

Additionally, if you have access to the audio version of a book, you can follow along as you read silently, which will improve your listening and pronunciation. Finally, your vocabulary will likely improve quickly, because most authors will repeat certain words and phrases that are relevant to their story or their main point.

In my experience, few sources of content are as versatile as books in their ability to sharpen your language skills. And yes this includes many sophisticated apps and software.

The only problem with using books to improve your language is that it can be difficult to do the first time you do it. There will be many unknown words and concepts that you don't understand that may frustrate you. How can you start to get the most out of your books and benefit from all of the potential language growth within? Read below for some general advice on this topic.

How to Break into Books

Start with books that you are familiar with in your target language. In a world filled with an endless amount of content, it can feel like a waste of time to experience something like a book a second or even a third time. But in the context of learning a language, we have to remember that repetition is our friend. When it comes to reading books, there is no exception.

Choosing to read a book that you have already read in your native language will give your mind the ability to focus on the language and not the story or the author's advice.

Use the one sentence method. The first time you read a book in another language it will probably be very slow. The number of unfamiliar words, characters, descriptions etc. can be extremely overwhelming when you see them all together on a page for the first time. One way to make reading your first few books in your target language more manageable is to read **one sentence at a time.**

By reading one sentence at a time you can deliberately pace yourself in your reading, which will provide you with the opportunity to analyze what you have read in a more systematic way. This is especially helpful if you tend to be a fast reader in your native language, as it prevents you from just reading the words on the page while potentially skipping over the details of the language that the author used.

The one sentence method is easy to do. Read one sentence and after you have read it, ask yourself the following questions to check you understanding:

- Did I understand the message that the author meant to convey?
- Did the sentence contain new or vaguely familiar vocabulary or grammar structures?

- Are there a significant number of new vocabulary terms that I don't know?

Taking the time to ask yourself and answer these questions will not only help you stay engaged in reading, but it will also allow you to pinpoint and correct any areas of weakness that you still may have with certain grammar concepts or word usages in the language.

If you take the time to do this early on while reading your book, you will find that the read will become easier as the words and certain grammatical structures begin to repeat themselves. Eventually, you will be able to begin reading at a faster pace than before, eliminating the need to stop at all when you do so.

Dealing with unfamiliar vocabulary and grammar. As I stated in one of the "things to avoid" sections of the Intermediate Level chapter, wanting to look up **every** unknown word can seriously slow down your progress. This is especially true when you begin to read books in your chosen language. Stopping during every line to look up a word, even if it is just a tap of a button or two to access an online dictionary, greatly interrupts the flow of your reading. It can also prolong the amount of time that it takes to complete the book.

The first full book that I completed in Spanish took me about a month to read, and in reality I probably was only able to absorb only half of what I read. This was partially due to the fact that I was still improving my reading skills, but also because I stopped to look up **most** words that I didn't know (which were numerous), and that slowed me down further.

My experience with that book lead me to develop the method that describe below, which helped me better balance reading with my dealings with unfamiliar grammar constructions and vocabulary terms.

My Method: The Second Look. What is my method? It's nothing complicated, but it does require some restraint and patience to use effectively. Instead of stopping to look up every word or phrase that I was unfamiliar with, **I began to only look them up if I read them a second time in the context of the book.**

I found that this simple strategy gave my mind a chance to **infer** the meaning of the word or phrases in the context that it was presented in.

Before coming up with this method, I would immediately research any word or phrase that I didn't know as I read. Naturally, I would read the definition, but not work to **learn or memorize it**, because, of course, I was going to continue reading, and probably encounter a new unknown word within a few lines or so. Then the process would repeat itself. The result was that my mind became overwhelmed with all of the new terminology and grammar that I was throwing at it all at once, and most times I closed the book feeling frustrated and, worse yet, having learned very few words!

Using the "second look method" it became easier for me to stay connected with what I was reading and focus on the message that I was reading and less on individual words. It also gave my subconscious time to learn the definition of the new word from the context. Most of the time after looking up the word later on, I found that the definition that I had guessed from context after encountering it for the first time was usually correct.

One word of caution with this technique If you can't understand **at least 50%** of the sentence that you are reading, it probably won't work very well, because you most likely won't understand the context of the entire sentence. This means it will be difficult to extract the meaning of unknown individual words. If this is the case, then you will definitely need to use a dictionary to clarify the meaning of some of the words, but you shouldn't worry about looking **all** of them up. You probably won't remember all of the definitions that you read immediately anyway.

While you may be saying, "but what if I don't see the word a second time!? What do I do!?" There will of course be many times when certain words don't present themselves a second time. If that occurs, then you just have to let it go.

I told you this technique requires restraint and patience. It also requires that you trust your brain to do what it has evolved to do, which is fill in gaps of information that are important for it.

Trust me, if you have come this far in learning a particular language, your brain knows that any sounds or words associated with it are important to you, and it will continue to work on the meaning of that word or phrase long after you've closed the book and gone to sleep. So much so that, the next time you encounter the word even if it's days later, it will probably immediately jump out at you. However, by then you would have already inferred its meaning, eliminating the need to look it up in a dictionary at all. Trust yourself, and try this technique to get more out of your reading sessions, I think you'll be pleasantly surprised at the results you get from it.

Read blogs, magazines, or other specialized materials. Now that you have mastered most of the basics of the language, you can and should branch out to more specialized topics. Perhaps, you've had a particular hobby or interest that you want to know more about, or you've been curious about a cultural aspect that involves your language, that you have yet to look into.

Connecting with people and organizations through various social media outlets, or if you are more old-school, subscribing to blogs, magazines and other regularly updated content can be a great way to learn terms that are more technical and improve your reading at the same time.

It can also provide some much needed variety among your reading sources and prevent you from hitting a content plateau.

Things to Avoid: Advanced Reading

Expecting to read for enjoyment (when beginning to read more complex materials). Since you will be able to read fairly well at this point, it can be easy to get ahead of yourself and go and grab that latest best seller or that classic work of literature that you always wanted to read in your target language. I highly advise against this.

If reading still requires effort at this point, you probably won't be able to appreciate the subtleties of the characters, messages, descriptions, themes etc. of those books right now. You will most likely have to stop often to look up words and certain phrases, and that will greatly distract you from the real essence of the book.

Find something that interests you, but save your reading of that master work for later when your skills have improved and you can actually enjoy it without worrying about not understanding a large portion of the contents of the book.

Stopping to look up EVERY UNKNOWN WORD. Even though we've discussed this at length and strategies to prevent from doing it, I think it is important to mention it here again primarily because the amount of unknown words that you encounter will probably be even higher than at the intermediate level when you start reading books. Bottom line, don't do it!

Not reading challenging materials. I know how daunting it can be to pick a large book that contains no words in your native language for the first time. When I did it for the first time, it made me want to go back to the simpler sentences and formats that I had become used to in other language tools.

It is imperative that you continue to challenge yourself with materials that will expand your knowledge of the language. Whether something is "hard" or "easy" will depend on how well you have trained yourself up to this point. Furthermore, you **should** know how to tell when something is too easy for you or is beyond the reach of your skills if you are truly at an advanced level in the language.

If you are at the point where you have even considered reading an entire book or other piece of long-form continuous content in your target language, I would argue that there a few materials that are beyond your reach, even though it may feel like they are. **Have confidence in the amount of the language that you do know and you will be surprised at the level of materials that you are ready for.**

Reading more challenging materials is the fastest way to improve your reading and your overall language skills, so you should at least try to attempt any materials that appear too difficult at first glance. After this is attempt, if you feel like the level of effort that you have to put in to comprehend and extract value from it is not worth it, then reassess your LCL and return to easier materials if necessary.

Reading books, websites, etc. that are popular but don't interest you - Most likely, reading is still work for you at this point in your studies. Don't sabotage yourself by choosing to read something that won't maintain your interest, just because it's on some list of books that you "have to read" in your language.

The only "bad" materials at this point are those not aimed at native speakers and materials that are not interesting to you. It doesn't matter how well-written or culturally significant it is, if it's boring to you, you won't get much out of it. So don't force yourself to read the *Harry Potter* series in your target language, just because it has been translated into 68 languages if you have never had any interest in it.

Not staying with materials long enough. The amount of content available online is mind-blowing. The virtually endless number of options can make it difficult to commit to one book, social media feed, or website for an extended amount of time. However, this constant availability of novelty can be harmful to your progress in the long-run.

Advanced Level

As I have mentioned before, it is very beneficial to stay with one reading source.

Therefore, I recommend choosing no more than **2** reliable sources for reading at one time (especially if they are books) and focusing on them exclusively. Then, after you complete one, move on to another one for continued practice.

In our fast-paced world, it will be difficult to do this because new suggestions for content are always bombarding us from all sides, but your commitment will be rewarded in the long-run.

Action Items for Advanced Learners: Advanced Speaking

At this point, you are probably able to use your language freely and naturally, even if only in short bursts. You may have even developed deeper relationships with your speaking abilities. If this is the case, congratulations! Now that you can communicate well in your language, it's time to take things to the next level with the following suggestions.

Take your language skills on the road

If you're someone who only speaks your language at home with friends or does self-talk (which we will discuss in greater detail shortly), then using your language in a public setting is a great way to move out of your comfort zone and force yourself to improve.

This will give you even more confidence to actually use your language with native speakers and other people that you don't know. It can be intimidating to do this at first, but if you've followed the instructions in this book so far, I assure you that your vocabulary, grammar, and tongue (muscle memory) are good enough to have at least a basic conversation with strangers.

If you are self-conscious about practicing with strangers, think of it as a fun game to see how people you can improve your skills. Additionally, in most cases you will probably never have to see that person again. So it's worth the risk of stumbling over your words or using questionable grammar to get additional practice. The only way to lose this game is to not play at all, so don't let shyness prevent you from reaching your goals!

In addition to talking to strangers, below are other suggestions for ways to refine and improve your speaking ability.

- **VOLUNTEER** locally at a place where your language is spoken. This will expose you to how people actually use the language on the street, plus it's always nice to give back and help others in need. Below are some places that regularly look for volunteers who speak different languages.
Local civic organizations for speakers of your target language - These might be cultural societies or organizations designed to help people who have recently immigrated. This a great way to help people from overseas get settled in a new place during what is usually a stressful time in their lives, while using your language skills.

Advanced Level

Tutoring kids or others in your native language in order for them to help you with your target language. There are several language exchange apps and websites that allow you to practice a language in exchange for helping someone else with your native language. You can also find some programs through local libraries or through the civic organizations mentioned above.

Community service events. Many communities hold events like bake sales, parades, job fairs etc. that need volunteers that can speak languages that are spoken in the community. This is a great way to practice and possibly network for a language job in the future.

- **Take a trip to a country or location where your language is spoken.** I suggested this earlier as a way to escape any learning plateau that you encounter. However, this time as an advanced learner, you can go to the country and truly **live** the language. With your ability to speak the language fluently, you will be able to connect with its people and culture in a way that is unique to its citizens. Also, you will rapidly improve and strengthen areas of weakness, as you hear how certain utterances are made colloquially in the country.

But what is the best way to do this? You can probably think of someone that you know that lived abroad for a few years, and returned barely having absorbed any of the language. You don't want that to happen to you.

When I think about the period of time that I lived in Okinawa, I can mentally divide my experience there into two parts. During the first half, which was about

a year long, I primarily spent time with other Americans, frequenting mostly well-known tourist areas on the island. During my second year, I spent more time with locals and found more obscure locations that were purely "Oki."
Based on those experiences, here are my suggestions for getting the most out of your time overseas.

- **Make friends with a local.** One of the biggest challenges about living or traveling overseas is not knowing anyone. By befriending a person who is a native of the area, you will most likely earn instant access to the places where they go, which will typically be a place that forces you to use your language skills and allows you to meet their friends who are most likely locals as well.

    There are several methods to meet locals overseas, below are just a few ideas:

    - Connect with them through social media groups
    - Go on a tour of a tourist location, and speak to locals there
    - Experience the nightlife of the area and meet locals at bars, restaurants, and clubs
    - Arrange to stay with a host family
    - Take a language class in your target language in the country

- **Leave your native language bubble.** In most countries there are enclaves and areas where native speakers of certain languages gather to provide support for each other and maintain their culture.

These small, yet often tight-knit microsocieties are often the first refuge that people seek out when they are living or traveling in a foreign country for an extended amount of time.

The problem is that these communities often provide so much comfort and familiarity that we can completely forget that we are abroad and after months or years in the country, can barely say any words in the target language.

For this reason, it is imperative that you make sure to venture out of your native language bubble.

My suggestion is to start slow and plan to spend at least **one day out of the week outside of your native language bubble.** As you meet more locals and become more familiar with the area, you can increase that frequency.

What you do doesn't really matter, as long as it is not centered on cultural traditions that are a part of your native culture and exposes you to new aspects of the country and the history of the target language and way of life.

- **Try to save your native language for emergencies only.** It's no secret that English is the dominant language of the world right now and that trend does not appear to be slowing or stopping anytime soon. This means that, if your native language is English, it is very possible to travel to most places in the world and **not have to speak another language.**

For most people, this is convenient because they don't have to make any effort to learn another language. But you're not most people.

I know from first-hand experience how frustrating it can be to travel overseas with the desire to improve your language skills, only to be met by locals who not only could speak English well, but also had no desire to speak **their** language with me. This usually was not out of malice, it was usually due to the fact that they wanted to practice their English with a native speaker, just like I did.

This can be a difficult issue to address. How can you possibly improve with your language if nobody will speak it with you?

My advice is simple: Ask them nicely, and offer to help them with their English in exchange upfront.

You can say something like: "Hi, I'm studying Chinese, and I would really like to practice it with you. I can help you with your English if you want too."

I have used lines like this in the past with Japanese as well, and it has worked well for me. By explicitly stating that I want to exchange languages with this person, it tells them that I am serious about their language (because, most casual learners won't even be able to make this request), and also it tells them that they will be taken care of by being able to improve their English as well. Everybody wins.

Without a preface like this, you will probably just end up speaking English, which does not help improve your speaking skills in your target language. **Be bold and ask them!** You will find that

Advanced Level

most people will be happy to help you, if you **ask politely.**

I know traveling abroad is not an option for everybody due to the financial and time commitment that it requires. But if your schedule and budget allow for it you should take advantage of the trip to get some valuable practice. There are few activities that will improve your skills faster than speaking the language in an immersive overseas environment.

- **Speaking on your own.** While tutors, trips, and volunteering are excellent resources for improving your speaking abilities, they all can cost money. If money is an issue for you, you'll have to get creative with how you practice speaking. That's where some of the following techniques come in.
- **Anytime you read a book or anything with dialogue, speak in a different way for any characters that you encounter.** While this may seem strange at first, I assure you it will improve your speaking ability. When I was younger, I used to play a lot of Japanese role playing games (JRPGs). I would read each character's lines of dialogue at different pitches, speeds, or accents, depending on what that character looked like or how their dialogue was written. My Mom would come in and ask me, "Who are you talking to?" and I would reply, "Oh it's the game."
Little did I know, that this silly habit was laying the foundation for me to learn other languages in the future. You can benefit from this exercise too. It may feel awkward initially, but try it and watch your fluency and vocabulary grow by leaps and bounds.

The more you can let go of how someone might perceive you essentially talking to yourself and really commit to it, the more you will benefit from the activity.

It is particularly helpful if whatever you are reading has a lot of dialogue, because it allows you to simulate a conversation with all of its interjections and colloquialisms. This simulation can easily be transferred to real life conversations later on.

- **Shadowing.** I've mentioned shadowing in a previous chapter, and it is another awesome alternative for individual speaking practice. Speaking along with an audio recording improves your intonation, accent, and rhythm of speaking. For details on shadowing refer to the *"How to know when to move on"* section of Chapter 4: Intermediate Level.
- **Talk to yourself.** If in the extreme case where you have no access to recorded materials in your target language, then you can fall back on talking to yourself.

Although you may feel awkward at first, as long as you are practicing making the sounds in the language, the practice will be beneficial for you.

To do it, you can ask yourself questions, and answer them out loud, describe your surroundings, make future plans, have a fake conversation; the list is virtually endless of what you can talk to yourself about. If you are really at a loss for ideas you can also write a practice dialogue and read it out loud for additional writing practice.

Whenever you feel embarrassed about doing any of the above mentioned speaking activities, ask yourself this: Would I rather feel embarrassed here alone, or in front of native speakers when I actually may need or want to speak the language?

The choice is up to you, but remember that any form of speaking practice is better than not opening your mouth at all, and if one of your goals is native-level fluency in the language then speaking and making mistakes is the only way to get there. Ultimately, how you get there, doesn't really matter.

Things to Avoid: Advanced Speaking

Not using the language enough: afraid of making mistakes. This is the third time that I've mentioned this in this book. I've mentioned it so many times, because I've met a lot of people over the years who speak or want to be able to speak a second language, and in my experience, this is the number one issue that prevents them from improving.

You have probably gotten over this by now, but I know some perfectionists who tend to not practice speaking as much as they should because they want to sound perfectly correct whenever they do it. Continue to make mistakes and improve. That's the only way to eventually speak "perfectly."

You've come so far, don't allow perfectionism to prevent you from fulfilling your goals.

Not self-evaluating. Now that you have a good amount of experience with the language, most people (including native speakers) will assume that you are fluent even if you are only able to produce a few utterances of organic speech in short bursts. This can be intimidating initially, because you no longer will want to fall back on the safety net of telling yourself things like "I'm just a beginner" or "I can't say much." You're the real deal now, and it's time to own it.

Additionally, speaking relatively fluently means two things:

- Areas of weakness in your skills won't improve unless you go out of your way to practice them
- Fewer people will correct your mistakes

This can be a great confidence boost at first. However, if you've developed bad habits in your pronunciation or word usage, you are less likely to find out about your mistakes from an external source. At this advanced level, small unnoticed mistakes will become extremely difficult to correct and detect, which can be frustrating for you and anyone else who you talk to.

This means that you must become even more critical of yourself when it comes to speaking. For some people who already scrutinize themselves regularly, this won't be much of a problem. But others have the exact opposite problem. They tend to dive into a new language and have great success speaking early on, but later on, they have a problem occasionally looking in the mirror and evaluating themselves for potential flaws and bad habits.

If you are one of the latter types of people, you should take extra care to evaluate your speaking regularly.

One of the ways you can hold yourself accountable is by recording yourself and listening critically. Ask yourself the following questions during your review of the recordings:

Advanced Level

- How's my pronunciation?
- Can I understand what I was trying to say?
- How can I improve?
- Did I produce the speech effortlessly, or am I still having a hard time pronouncing certain things?

These are just a few of the questions that can ask yourself. If you don't feel like you can objectively evaluate your performance on your own, enlist the help of a friend, tutor, or partner to listen to you speak and give you feedback. This can further increase the accuracy of your evaluation and help hold you accountable for mistakes.

Not learning idioms. "He's six feet under." "It was a sticky situation." "She waited until the situation blew over." These are all examples of idioms in the English language.

Idioms are a big part of every language. They often carry heavy cultural significance of the the society that the language is connected to; therefore, it can be vital to understand how idioms are used in various contexts among native speakers. While knowing a few idioms does not mean you are fluent in a language, if you are able to appropriately implement them in conversations with native speakers, they will **always** be impressed with you and assume that you are fluent.

One of the difficult things about learning language idioms is that, many are so nuanced, that they can only be applied to a certain scenario or occurrence, which makes them difficult to encounter and to implement in casual speech. Of course, some widely spoken languages, like Spanish, have idiom resources that have thousands of them listed, but just reading them and memorizing them would not be very helpful in actually learning how and when it would be most appropriate to use them.

So what's the best way to learn idioms?

By far the best way to learn them right now, is to read articles and watch videos online. This way, you will find the most appropriate way that the idiom is currently being used, and what type of people use them. The last thing you want to do is learn an outdated expression that was in style over 50 years ago, that only people from an older generation would be able to understand.

After you've found a few examples of the idiom, do some additional research about it online. You may possibly find a native speaker who has written specifically about that saying and provides additional details about how native speakers use it, its linguistic origins, or other pieces of valuable information. I did this with many idioms in Spanish, and I learned a great deal about the evolution of the Spanish language and culture in the process.

While you may not know many idioms at this point, it would be to your benefit to learn some of the more common phrases. If you learn even a few, I assure you that any native speaker will instantly be impressed, even if you are not that fluent.

Advanced Level

Action Items for Advanced Learners: Advanced Listening

Get away from materials that are focused on teaching your target language (even if they are in the target language). In the early stages of your training, you probably listened to materials that were specifically designed to <u>teach</u> you the language. Most of these resources provided audio that was suitable for beginners and maybe even intermediate learners, but probably weren't designed to help you beyond that.

Now at this advanced level, you can use **anything** you want as a listening resource. This should be the moment that you've be waiting for, the ability to understand almost anything in your target language that you want! On the other hand this can often be very intimidating, because you may not be sure that if you start watching that show in Hindi that you always dreamed of watching without subtitles, you may not be able to get much value out of it, because you can't understand most of it. I experienced this same feeling when studying Spanish.

If you are still not feeling confident about your ability to benefit from and possibly even enjoy listening to native level content in your target language, then read on below for how to better approach and eventually conquer it once and for all.

Movies, TV Series, Radio, and Podcasts

This category includes any audio in your target language that was recorded for native speakers of that language, in that particular language.

Below is a step-by-step process to make the content more approachable for you.

Begin to watch movies and programs in your target language with subtitles in the target language at first if you need them. Subtitles are can be a helpful confidence boost, but as I mentioned before, if you want to focus on training your ears, turn the subtitles off. You will improve your listening much faster this way.

Try repeating words and phrases that are unfamiliar to you or write them down as you watch and/or listen. This will help you highlight the unknown words or phrases in your mind and make it easier for you to recognize them next time you hear them.

Focus on the context of when certain words and phrases are used by native speakers. One of the great things about listening to content recorded for native speakers is that you can not only train your listening skills, but you will improve your word usage as well because you will see/hear when it is most appropriate to use certain words and phrases.

Advanced Level

Focus on the cultural context of the material (time period, famous historical figures, customs/traditions of the culture etc). This knowledge expands your awareness of the culture that is connected with the language. It also will help you with word usage issues as well.

Be prepared to watch the material more than once to solidify your understanding of the speech used. When you first begin to watch or listen to content for native speakers, be prepared to listen or watch the same recording multiple times. During the first time, choose one or two of the above activities to focus on. Then the second time, focus on something else. It all depends on how you want to do it. But you should not try to do everything at once, especially the first time. You will most likely get overwhelmed and gain little from it.

Suggested progression of materials to watch or listen to for listening practice

While I believe that you should focus on material that is interesting and relevant to you, realize that recordings that are dubbed tend to be easier to start with than materials that were originally produced in your target language. I explain my reasoning for this below.

Programs dubbed into the target language were originally recorded in your native language, so the language used will often closely reflect the syntax and tone of the original recording. This is helpful when you first begin to take advantage of content in your target language because, the way the language is used and structured will probably be more familiar to you, thus making it easier to understand and learn from.

An example of this would be an American movie originally filmed in English, is dubbed into Mandarin Chinese so that native Chinese speakers can watch and enjoy it. This would be a good resource for a native English speaker to utilize for improving his or her Mandarin, because they will most likely be familiar with the setting, word usage, and style of speaking used in the movie, since it was originally filmed in English.

Additionally, dubbed materials are typically recorded by professionals that tend to use clear pronunciation and clean audio, so it's the perfect place to begin watching and even enjoying materials in your target language.

Programs originally recorded or filmed in the target language are more challenging because you will most likely not understand the full context of the story, and the speech patterns may be more difficult to follow.

For example, a Japanese film originally recorded in Japanese would require a deeper understanding of Japanese culture and language syntax for a student of Japanese, than a movie **dubbed** into Japanese from another language.

Use the strategies above to slowly increase your comprehension. The first time that you are able to watch a full movie or listen to a full podcast or radio program completely in your target language and understand it, you will know that your listening ability and understanding in the language is very high.

The Pros and Cons of Using Music for Listening Practice

Is it helpful to use music to learn a foreign language? The answer depends greatly on who you ask. I'm a big music fan, so when I was younger, it was one of my go to sources of audio input. However, now I tend to stay away from using it, especially if I am beginning to learn a new language from scratch. I will use my personal experience as a framework to discuss why I made this shift in outlook towards music as an effective language tool, then I'll use that as a foundation to discuss the pros and cons of using music to learn a foreign language.

Pro 1: Repetitiveness. As you know by now, repetition is a key factor in learning any language. The generally repetitive nature of music is one of the traits that makes it such a fantastic audio source. Most song lyrics contain an unchanging chorus that is repeated usually 3 or 4 times throughout the duration of the track. This makes it easy to learn those words very rapidly, since you will probably listen to the song multiple times if you like it.

Pro 2: Emotional Connection. Remember back at the beginning of Chapter 3 when we discussed the elements of boosting your memory to learn more vocabulary? The emotional element of memory is one of the elements that can be greatly utilized when listening to music.

If you are able to establish an emotional connection with a particular song, through its lyrics or through the unique circumstances when you personally encountered or listened to the song, then you will probably never forget the words associated with it.

I still remember the words the lyrics of some of the first songs that I heard when I first began studying Japanese by groups and artists like Dragon Ash and Utada Hikaru. As of this publication, that was almost fifteen years ago! That's how powerful music can be!

Con 1: Lyrics can be difficult to understand. This is the primary reason that I decided not to discuss music until the Advanced chapter and why I personally do not use music as much as a way to improve my listening skills. **Music can be too difficult to truly appreciate for a beginner in a language.** Outside of the chorus, which is repeated multiple times, the rest of the lyrics of the song will be more difficult to grasp for a new learner of that language. This is not just because of the often hypnotic beats or instrumentation, but also because of the language usage itself.

Song lyrics are often molded to fit within the melody and musicality of the track. The result is that certain words and expressions and phrases can be shortened or eliminated completely just to preserve the rhythm of the song. What does this mean to you? Ultimately, this means that unless you plan to listen to the same song hundreds of times, you will probably not be able to understand most of the lyrics without careful analysis of them.

Furthermore, artists tend to use a lot of idioms and slang that will fly over the heads of most beginners learning any language. Even if you are able to ascertain the meaning of the slang using the context of the lyrics, the nuance and true cultural impact will more difficult to appreciate without much exposure to the culture. This is experience with the language that typically only people who have spent months or years with the language possess.

Con 2: The Focus is Often Not on the Language. Music has multiple elements to its structure. Most songs contain multiple instruments, voice samples, and other elements that take the focus off of the lyrics, which is what you should be concerned with as a student of that language. This is another reason why I stopped using music as a language learning resource.

As you can probably tell from this section, I am more than just a casual fan of music. As the son of a former radio DJ, music has been a part of my life from an early age, and it is truly one of my passions. So in a way it pains me to discourage other language learners from using it to get more proficient with their language of choice.

With my background of listening to music from all around the world, it is simply too difficult for me to focus on the linguistic characteristics of a song. The beat, instrumentation, and overall feeling of a song, all pull me in and contribute to my enjoyment of it, yet simultaneously distract from the potential educational value that the song may have for me.

The Verdict on Music as a Listening Resource. I have read and heard accounts of people who have learned a foreign language almost exclusively by listening to music. If you are someone who has been able to do this, then I congratulate you on your achievement. But I would argue that the majority of people will not be able to learn exclusively through this method. Music is designed to pull us in multiple directions through a myriad of factors, and the words are just one of those characteristics that can draw our attention. As a student of a foreign language, the words should be your primary concern.

Music can be enjoyable to consume, but in my opinion, it generally is not a reliable language teacher. However, it can help with cultural familiarity and certain slang in a language, if you have enough knowledge and exposure to the language and the way of life associated with it to be able to take advantage of it as the potentially powerful language tool that it can be.

Things to Avoid: Advanced Listening

Using subtitles in your native language. You shouldn't need them anymore at this point, and they will make it more difficult for you to focus on your target language.

Avoid being distracted by the narrative of TV series, movies etc., and not focusing on the language. Be aware that a TV show/online series or movie that you began to watch for listening practice can quickly absorb you in its story and characters and distract you from paying attention to the language. **Stay focused when you watch or listen.**

You can (and should) set aside time to enjoy media in your target language, but it should not be during your designated study time. **Set aside certain series/movies/media etc. for language growth and others for pure enjoyment.** This way, you will be able to focus more easily when you are in language learning mode and relax more when you are watching or listening for leisure.

Passive listening. I've mentioned passive listening before, but I will restate it here. Since you are at a higher level and can understand more now you may think you can get away with it, but it's not effective for improving your listening skills. Staying engaged while listening will help your skills grow quickly.

Focusing on what you don't know, instead of what you do know.

It can be difficult and demoralizing to watch an entire movie and only understand half of what happened in it. This **will** happen often during your first few months of dealing with native materials. **This is normal and you shouldn't let it demotivate you about the progress that you've already made.**

If you obsess too much about how much of the audio you **can't understand,** you will miss out on the parts that you **do understand**, which will slow down your progress. Expect to not understand everything all the time, but set a goal for yourself to learn a certain amount of new words or phrases every time you listen. This can add some structure to your listening sessions and allow you to relax and just listen after you've met your goal.

Action Items for Advanced Learners: Advanced Writing

In my opinion, writing is the easiest aspect of language to improve, and it's not just because I like to write. It's because writing can be done anywhere, silently, and without a partner. It usually doesn't cost any money to practice, **and you can get immediate feedback on your performance by**

copy and pasting what you wrote into an online translator and seeing if it makes sense.

Despite this, if you desire to elevate your writing skills to a higher level in your target language you will have to improve your **vocabulary** and **do more advanced and technical reading** than you have done up to this point. This is in addition to just writing more in general. Below are a few suggestions on how you can improve your writing even further and take it a level that a high school or collegiate level educated native speaker would possess.

Join a group forum online. Consider joining a forum online that forces you to communicate in your target language. With social media, it is very easy to find a community on any platform, of speakers that not only speak your target language, but have specialized interests as well. It could be as general as sports or as specific as fly fishing, but no matter what your interest is, there's probably a group out there for you. When you find this group, force yourself to write in your language as much as possible when communicating with other members.

Pay special attention to **specialized terminology** or **jargon** that your chosen community uses, and challenge yourself to incorporate those words into your writing. This will be key to solidifying them into your mind and in your writing.

Write blog posts. Writing a blog post about something that is interesting to you is a great way to publicly practice more advanced writing. There are thousands of websites that will allow you to write a guest post on their site, or better yet, if you feel bold enough you can start your own blog and write whatever you want on it.

By publicly displaying your writing online, you will automatically become more critical of your work, which will force you to improve more rapidly, than if you were writing for yourself.

I personally used this technique to practice my Spanish writing on Medium.com. Medium is a blogging website that allows anyone to write blog posts and connect with other writers in the process, so basically it's a social media site for writers.

Although admittedly, all of my writing didn't have perfect grammar or word usage, it was enough for a few native Spanish speakers to notice and provide me with positive feedback. This greatly increased my confidence and made me feel like I could move on to even more advanced writing in Spanish, like writing a book.

Practice for a writing test. When's the last time you took a high school or collegiate level exam? A few months? Or may more than a "few" years? Whether it has been only a few months or decades since your last test, practicing for one of these tests is great writing practice, provided that the test contains a written component that you can use for practice.

The advantage of doing writing test prep from a test preparation book, website, or app is that you will be forced to inject structure and some level of analysis into your writing. These two writing traits are universal among educated native speakers of any language.

Most books or websites may contain reading passages that you must analyze before providing a response, or they may provide a topic that requires you to do some research before you can formulate an answer. Either scenario will be beneficial for improving your writing at an advanced level.

For some languages that are widely spoken like Spanish, it will be very easy to find these types of materials online or in print. There are so many students in the U.S. that speak Spanish, that in some cases, certain standardized academic test like the General Education Development (GED) test are offered completely in that language.

However, if your language is less common, you may have to look harder for educational materials that have been produced for students in that language. Luckily, you can easily find and probably order these materials online with a quick search or visit a website in your target language and take advantage of any writing prompts or information provided there. This will allow you to practice reading and give you greater cultural insight into how a country that speaks that language organizes their educational materials, in addition to providing writing practice.

Things to Avoid: Advanced Writing

Not receiving feedback. Just like with speaking, it is easy to develop bad habits with writing, especially if you have mostly practiced in isolation from any form of feedback. I know writing can be very personal to some people, but if you want to improve, allowing someone else to review your work and provide feedback is the best thing you can do to improve your writing.

There are multiple websites like italki, LingQ, and many others that allow you to submit writing samples and receive feedback from native speakers. If that seems too intimidating for you consider seeking out someone that you trust like a tutor, teacher, or close friend that knows how to write in the language, to give you honest and gentle feedback.

Studying Culture

You have no doubt picked up some of the culture of your target language at this point, but now you should begin to pay more attention to it as an advanced learner. Culture and language have a close relationship with each other. A change in one can often be seen in the other, which contributes to the evolution of language. With the rapid advancement of technology, and the widespread use of the internet all around the world, which began in the first two decades of the 21st century, the lines between certain cultures became increasingly blurred. The result was that many cultures influenced each other; thus, their languages changed too.

Now it's not uncommon to hear certain English words with Japanese pronunciation in Japan. Words like *suupaa*) (supermarket) or *depaato* (department store) are widely used in Japan.

Changes is social trends and technology can also influence culture. For example, in English, the words "selfie" or "vlog" were not widely known or used at all 10 or 15 years ago, yet the spread in popularity of technology has made them common words today. Similar evolutions are occurring everyday around the world in many languages. This most likely includes your target language as well.

Right now, it is easier than it has ever been to become familiar with the culture of your target language. Most of the time a quick search online will lead you to videos, blogs, magazines, and other materials for you to read, watch, or experience in the language. For more suggestions on expanding your cultural horizons, read below.

- **Watch documentaries (in your target language if possible).** Documentaries are a gold mine of cultural knowledge. Most of the time they cover one topic in depth, which is great for your personal historical knowledge, and valuable fodder for relating to native speakers on a deeper level. This is especially true if it concerns common knowledge that most native speakers are taught in school when they are young.
Additionally, most of them contain a good mix of interviews with experts related to that subject and everyday people who may be somehow involved with the story. This will expose you to both formal and informal language at the same time, further expanding your options when communicating in the language.
- **Watch a series in your target language.** As I mentioned before, most TV series made in your target language will reflect the cultural values associated with that language. This makes them valuable resources for getting exposure to how

native speakers of that language think and see themselves as a people, nation, or culture.

- Wondering how to get more culture out of a TV or web series in your target language? Some questions to ask yourself that might help are:
- What are the motivations of the characters?
- What do they value?
- How are those values different from my culture?
- What themes seem prevalent throughout the series
- What are the sources of conflict in the story and how are they resolved?
- What brings the characters joy?
- What culture-specific activities do the characters engage in? How are those activities similar or completely different as compared to your culture?

By thinking about some of these questions as you watch, you will be better prepared to engage with native speakers of the language. Furthermore, you can take advantage of this activity a step further by asking a native speaker questions about certain aspects of the series that confused you or that you want more information about.
I did this often with music and certain Japanese dramas when I lived in Japan, and I usually gained more insight from a Japanese local than I would have if I had looked exclusively online. This was especially true if the series or song was very popular among locals.

- **Read articles or books about historical and current events in your target language.** History is a fantastic source of cultural knowledge, but current events occurring in a region where your language is spoken can be just as culturally significant. With the abundance of news sources available, it can be overwhelming to try to keep up with all of the current events going on in a particular country or region, but it is worth it to understand how those events may be shaping the people who speak your target language.

  I recommend reading **one** or **two** news articles a day from a country or region that speaks your target language. You can focus on one country or region for a few weeks or a month and then move on to another. If you do this consistently for a few months, eventually you will have a mental map of the general situation in several major geographic regions where your target language is spoken from the perspective of a native speaker.
- **Travel abroad.** This builds on the advice in the previous paragraph and on the information in the "How to get the most out of traveling abroad" section found earlier in this chapter. Traveling and/or living in an environment where your language is spoken is by far the best way to experience and absorb the culture in the most natural way possible.
- **Don't just go overseas and stay at the fancy resort and go to the tourist hot spots.** Try and carve out time to experience life the way locals do in some way (within reason of course). This could be going to a market, trying dishes that are common to the area,

Advanced Level

or attending a culturally significant event that is off the beaten path, but has great cultural significance to locals. There are many ways to do it.

The point is to make use of your time in the best way possible and of course use and improve your language skills as much as you can in the process. Your goal is to learn the culture from the perspective of a native speaker of your language. This will improve your knowledge of the language and make it easier for you to talk with native speakers of the language about things that matter to them.

Avoid learning the language in a vacuum of grammar books and language apps, and get out there and live the language!

Sample Study Plans for Advanced Learners

As in the previous chapters, I recommend splitting up your language learning at the advanced level into two days at this level. Below is a sample learning schedule:

Day 1

- **Vocab Study/Review.** Review any words encountered on the previous day(s): **15%**
- **Listening/Culture.** These go well together. You may want to listen once for language comprehension, then a second time to focus on the cultural aspects: **35%**
- **Reading/Speaking.** Reading tends to take a long time, especially at the beginning of this level, so plan to spend a lot of time reading SLOWLY. You will prioritize reading here, but you will naturally practice speaking if you read aloud: **50%**

Day 2

- **Vocab Study/Review.** Review any words encountered on the previous day(s): **15%**
- **Listening/Culture.** 20%
- **Writing.** 15%
- **Speaking/Reading.** These can be done together if you have no one or nowhere to practice. If you have access to a tutor, teacher, or friend, try to speak with them on these days rather than reading: **50%**

Things to Avoid: Advanced Study Schedule

All of the same pitfalls from the Intermediate level apply here. Here's a quick reminder of what they are:

DON'T

- Try to study too many things in one day
- Try to focus on more than one modality at a time
- Look up EVERY word in a dictionary **all** the time
- Be too hard on yourself

Estimated Length Of Time At the Advanced Level?

Approximately 7 months - 1 year. The time that you spend as advanced speaker, will depend largely on your long term goals with the language. If you are still actively improving your language at this level, you most likely have a goal that extends further than being fluent in the language.

The kind of language proficiency and literacy that will allow you to obtain employment and live comfortably in a country that speaks your target language does not come easily, and will most likely require you to have official proof that you can speak and understand the language at a high level. For some countries like Finland, Korea, and Germany it is a requirement that you have at least satisfactory knowledge of their languages to be able to do business there. Yes languages are that important to some countries!

While 7 months to a year on top of the time that it took for you to reach this level of proficiency in the language may feel like a long time, it's probable that the time will feel more bearable during this period. This is because you can more or less get by with the language, and you won't have to be as deliberate with adhering to study techniques or a rigid study schedule. You will be sharpening your skills unconsciously as you absorb native materials and interact with native speakers of the language, which hopefully, were some of the reasons why you decided to learn it in the first place.

How to Know When to Move On To the Next Level?

Think you're almost ready to call yourself a native-like speaker? Start by reassessing your LCL. How's it going? If you have a Language Confidence Level of at least **28/35**. You might be ready to move on. (SEE THE PREVIOUS CHAPTER FOR MEASURING YOUR LANGUAGE CONFIDENCE LEVEL.)

This is something that I will discuss more in-depth in a section about language credentialing, but I believe that formally testing your skills is essential to knowing that you have reached native level proficiency. Being tested by an objective testing entity goes a long way in convincing yourself and others that you truly understand the language at a high level.

Therefore, you should aim to test yourself in each of the language modalities that are applicable to your goals (speaking, listening, reading, writing) in some way before classifying yourself as a native-like speaker of any

Advanced Level

language. Based on the outcome of the test, it will be a strong indicator of how proficient you are in that area.

The "test" doesn't have to be evaluated in the traditional sense to be effective, but it should provide a challenge for your skills outside of your personal study environment. Below are some examples.

Testing your Speaking

An effective speaking test should evaluate more than just your fluency in a language. It should also test your ability to sound natural and pleasing to native speakers, doing your best to avoid awkward pauses or the need to ask for clarification by the person or machine that is listening to you. To put it simply, the language should flow out of you **almost** as effortlessly as it does in your native language.

Remember, being a competent speaker of a language does **not** always mean needing to have a large vocabulary of words. It means being able to convey your thoughts, desires, or needs to someone else in a way that makes sense to them.

With that said, below are a few ways that you can test your speaking:

- **Applying for a job** in which the language is needed and doing well during an evaluation
- Taking an any oral exam
- Traveling abroad and being able to live your life smoothly without worrying to much about using the language

Testing your Listening

Good listening skills are required in order to have any conversations with native speakers, so you may be able to test them in tandem with your speaking skills. However, many official exams test the two skills separately, which will cause you to have to focus exclusively on your listening skills.

By this point, if you've followed the action items in this book at some or all of the levels, you surely can recognize even minor differences between certain sound pronunciations in your target language with native speaker accuracy. The only things that may give you trouble are understanding certain notoriously thick accents or specific regionalisms/idioms that are only used by native speakers in small enclaves of the world.

When I traveled to Singapore in the fall of 2018, I sometimes had trouble understanding some of my girlfriend's friends. Although they speak English as an official language as well over there, they tend to speak the British variant as opposed to the American variant of English. Additionally, they have developed their own accent (which is influenced by several different languages and cultures) that is unique to Singapore. The result of all of this was that I sometimes had difficulty understanding some of them when they spoke English, even though I am also a native speaker.

While you may not be able to understand every variant of your target language, it takes considerable experience and exposure to the language to be able to discern different dialects and accents of a language. Therefore, if the scenario described above applies to you with your target language, then you are most likely prepared to excel at nearly any evaluation of your listening skills.

Here are a few suggestions of how you can evaluate your listening skills:

- Taking an oral or listening exam
- Traveling to a place where the language is spoken and engaging in a conversation with locals
- Applying for a job where you have to use your language

Testing your Reading

Being able to speak in a foreign language is impressive, but but being able to read well in it is almost more so in my opinion. This is because most language learners focus on fluency as their primary objective. I don't know many people who learn a language just to be able to read it well. Nevertheless, reading is an extremely useful skill that many language learners overlook. Here are some ways that you can evaluate your reading skills at a high level:

- Taking an exam in the target language
- Translating materials vocally in real time as you travel for other people
- Reading an entire piece of literature or non-fiction in your target language

Testing your Writing

Much like reading, writing is typically shrugged off as a "nice to have but not necessary" skill to have with a foreign language. I can understand why. Most language learners will not have a use for it; as being able to hold a relaxing conversation with others in the language is their only goal. However, if you desire to be employed by a company that uses or works with others that use your target language, then writing will become extremely important.

You don't need to be able to draft stunning prose to be considered a good writer. The only thing that matters is general readability and a generally clear understanding of the grammar of the language. Notice I did not say flawless grammar. I have known many non-native speakers who make minor mistakes with using plurals, or have improper subject-verb agreement in their writing, and they were professionals who had spoken English for decades. Despite the errors, I still understood what they wrote, and I didn't think any less of them for it.

You will now be that non-native speaker in your target language that potentially makes mistakes with writing. If you want to find out if you are ready to use your writing in a more official way, then read some of my suggestions below on how you can test yourself.

- Taking an exam in the target language
- Using your language publicly in a formal way (writing in a blog, writing messages at work etc.) - *See section "Advanced Writing" for more details*
- Volunteer to do translating work

General Notes about the Advanced Level

Stay consistent with your studies! Even though you've come so far you still need to focus on improvement!

You should be able to enjoy yourself more during this phase. You are finally consuming materials and interacting openly with your language. You've earned it so you should enjoy it!

Don't forget to test yourself regularly to gauge your progress along the way. You can use some of the testing methods above, or refer to the "Plateau" section for ideas on how to challenge your skills and keep them as sharp as possible.

By the end of this level, you should be officially **fluent** in your language! Now you can tell your friends and put it on your resume without worrying about someone asking you to prove it (because you know you can speak, read, write, and understand it in many forms).

I can remember when I realized that I had become fluent and literate in Spanish. I felt excited and accomplished that I had achieved a goal that at one point I thought was impossible. The feeling also made me wonder if I could even be confused for a native Spanish speaker. The thought made me think about some of the differences between native and non-native speakers of a language, some of which we will discuss in further detail in the next chapter.

Advanced Level Quick Notes

DO (VOCABULARY)
- Continue to actively build your vocabulary
- Transition to using a reliable monolingual dictionary in your target language

DON'T (VOCABULARY)
- Neglect to build your vocabulary

DO (READING)
- Read the news
- Read books
- Read blogs, magazines, or other specialized materials

DON'T (READING)
- Expect to read for enjoyment (when beginning to read more complex materials)
- Stop to look up EVERY UNKNOWN WORD
- Read materials that are not challenging enough for your level
- Read books, websites, etc. that are popular but don't interest you
- Change reading materials with too much frequency

Advanced Level

DO (SPEAKING)

- Make more attempts to use your language publicly by doing a few of the following things:
    - Volunteering
    - Taking a trip to a country or location where you language is spoken, and using your language as much as possible there
    - Speaking by yourself
        - Roleplaying with different voices and accents
        - Shadowing
        - Talking to yourself about whatever you want

DON'T (SPEAKING)

- Be afraid to make mistakes and not use the language because of it
- Neglect to evaluate yourself
- Neglect to learn idioms

DO (LISTENING)

- Get away from materials that are focused on <u>teaching</u> your target language (even if they are in the target language)
- Watch and listen to movies, TV series, radio, podcasts and other sources for exposure to the language
    - Watch media with subtitles in the target language only if necessary
    - Repeat words and phrases that are unfamiliar to you and/or write them down as you watch or listen
    - Focus on the **situational** context of when certain words and phrases are used by native speakers
    - Focus on the **cultural** context of the material (time period, famous historical figures, customs/traditions of the culture etc.)
    - Be prepared to watch the material more than once to solidify your understanding of the speech used
    - Start with programs dubbed into your target language then move on to programs filmed or recorded originally in the target language
- Consider using music as a source for audio (although I don't recommend it for effective listening practice)

Advanced Level

DON'T (LISTENING)
- Use subtitles in your native language
- Be distracted by the narrative of the TV series, movies, and programs at the expense of on the language
- Listen passively to audio sources during designated study time
- Focus more on what you don't know, instead of what you do know

DO (WRITING)
- Join a group forum online and participate
- Write blog posts
- Practice for a writing test

DON'T (WRITING)
- Neglect to receive feedback

DO (STUDYING CULTURE)
- Watch documentaries (in your target language if possible)
- Watch a series in your target language. Ask yourself questions about the culture as you watch.
- Read articles, books, and other documents about historical and current events in your target language
- Travel abroad and interact with locals, visit culturally significant places, and get out and live the language!

DO (STUDY SCHEDULE)
- Divide your schedule into a two day alternating schedule

DON'T (STUDY SCHEDULE)
- Try to study too many things in one day
- Try to study more than one modality at a time
- Look up EVERY word in a dictionary all the time
- Be too hard on yourself

Native-Like Level (Chapter 6)

It's a little after noon and the sun is beating down on your face as you sip coffee in a small yet charming outdoor cafe in Granada. Suddenly, there's a soft tap on your shoulder and you turn around to see an elderly woman staring at you. The woman asks you in rapid-fire Spanish about the best place to eat in the area. It takes some effort for you to pull yourself away from chapter 7 of Don Quijote, but you put it down and begin to give her a detailed description of Cafe de los Suenos just a short walk down Calle La Calzada in Spanish. The woman asks you politely how you know the area so well, and your response is an abbreviated explanation of the circumstances that led to your remote company work in Nicaragua 6 months ago.

After a 15 minute exchange about other possibilities to eat and swapping opinions about what you both think about the state of Nicaraguan politics, the elderly woman begins to walk away, but before she does, she asks you, "De dónde eres?" (Where are you from?). After you tell her, her eyes light up with surprise. "Pensé que eras de aquí con la manera que hablas" (I thought you were from here with the way that you speak.)

You smile to yourself after she walks away and you settle your bill to prepare to get back to work. That's the fifth time that someone has mistaken you for a native speaker this week and you still aren't tired of it, even after 6 months.

Being a Native-Like Speaker

If you could at all relate to this short hypothetical scenario, then chances are you have reached the native-like level in your target language. Congratulations!! You really have achieved something that very few people in the world have on their own, without having grown up with contact in the language. Yes, you should feel extremely pleased with yourself for your accomplishment.

You might think that because you have reached the pinnacle of achievement in your language (being confused for a native speaker) that your journey with your target language is over. I'd argue that in some ways it is over, but in others it isn't.

In this chapter, we will discuss a few more strategies that will allow you to refine your language skills even more (yes there's still more you can do!), some harsh truths about being a non-native speaker of the language, and finally; a few additional tips for dealing with issues like language deterioration and maintenance.

Who Is A Person At The Native-Like Level?

Someone who can fully express their needs, desires, and thoughts with relative ease in the target language. This may or may not include being able to write and read in the language, it depends on the person's language goals.

Native-Like Level

Someone who **maintains** their language skills by consuming media and materials in their target language

Action Items for Native-Like Speakers

While you shouldn't have to follow a strict and formatted study plan at this point, there are still some things that you can do to further boost your skills. Below are a few suggestions.

Specialize. Now that you can communicate in the language effectively, you may want to consider adding a focus to your skills. Is there a particular niche or area of your work that would benefit from having specialized vocabulary? I know in the world of language interpretation, it is very common for interpreters to specialize in legal or medical vocabulary, for example.

A specialization will not only help you standout from others who just know the language, but you will also become more knowledgeable in general about that area. Below are some more ideas about specialization.

- Focus on a particular region or dialect that interests you and learn about it in depth
- Watch documentaries, read books, or articles online about the region (in your target language)
- Listen to podcasts about topics that interest you

Entertain yourself. After you reach native-like proficiency, it becomes very easy to integrate the

language into your life. Gone are the days when you had to keep your online dictionary tab open or pause recordings to try to process what you just heard. Now you should be able to enjoy most media, music, or anything else that you would want to experience completely in the target language as if it were your mother tongue.

The point is to engage with the language in some way everyday, even if it is only for a brief period. This will go a long way toward maintaining your skills.

BONUS NOTE **Add comedy and stand-up to your line up.** It may seem odd to watch a stand-up comedy routine in your target language performed by a comedian who you probably don't know. But in reality it is a great source of current slang, and surprisingly, of current events and social trends that are prevalent in that country or region. Comedians often don't hold back their opinions of social issues or other nuances of their society, so it is to your benefit to watch and learn about a side of culture that would only be available to you if you lived or were raised in that country or community. You will probably laugh at least a little bit too, even if you don't understand all of it.

As of this writing, Netflix is the king of stand-up comedy from most major areas around the globe. I'm sure you can find clips on YouTube, or other places online if you look hard enough. If you have the money, and want an unforgettably cultural experience, consider going to a live show in your area.

Become a master storyteller. One skill that really makes anyone who has learned a second language stand out is the ability to tell a story in that language. Think about the last time that you spent time in a casual non-work environment with someone that you shared a close relationship with. Chances are, they told you a story of some kind, or you told them a story.

Perhaps the story was about how you went to the store and ended up buying much more than you expected to and later dropped everything on the ground on the way to the car, because you were too cheap to buy plastic bags, (those from California will understand). Or maybe it was about a recent development in your relationship with your current boy/girlfriend.

Whatever the details of the story, it probably contained some or all of the following elements. Let's use the grocery store story as an example:

- Setting: The grocery store
- Participants: Just you and maybe a person who saw you drop everything
- Circumstance(s): You didn't want to pay for bags and decided to carry everything on your own
- What happened: You dropped everything on the ground
- Outcome/Resolution/Opinion: You were embarrassed and had to pick everything up as someone laughed in their car

If you think about the level of language that is necessary for you to produce a story that is at least complete, you will begin to realize why it is the gold-standard of a highly proficient language student. The level of language required becomes even more demanding if you are trying to tell a story that is interesting, compelling, funny, AND culturally relevant. This is why it is highly beneficial for you to pay attention to comedy, because you will see someone who has mastered this structure and can deliver it in a culturally relevant way. Here are a few of the language skills that are necessary for you to be able to tell outstanding stories in your language:

- <u>Be able to provide descriptions of</u>: Places, people, and events in the present, past, or future
- <u>Be able to improvise</u>: Knowledge of filler words and phrases, ability to quickly connect between relevant details and topics to your story
- <u>Be able to read social cues of your audience</u>: Understand the cultural and social cues that may be different from your culture. These may include facial expressions, verbal cues, gestures or any other way that the communication is different in the culture of your target language.
- <u>Be able to relate culturally to your audience</u>: Sufficient knowledge of culturally understable and relevant references to draw on for examples that your audience can relate to

These abilities represent the culmination of your ability in your target language, and often you must be able to perform them on cue, with little or no prior preparation or thought. If it seems extremely difficult to do this, that's because it is!

Without top notch language ability, your stories will be full of awkward pauses and unconnected utterances that will be difficult for the person or people listening to understand. When your audience begins to ask for clarifications that are not related to the context of the story, but to your language usage, then you have taken them out of the experience of your story and and most likely have lost their engagement. In order to prevent this from happening, the following are a few ways that you can practice becoming a master storyteller:

- **Start small.** Initially it will be difficult to tell a story the same way that a native speaker can. Your first few attempts to include all of the elements listed above will most likely be filled with pauses and stammering as you struggle to form your thoughts in rapid succession in a manner that makes sense. **Instead consider telling a story that at least has a beginning, middle, and an ending, to start with.** As you become more comfortable with including the basic structure of a story, it will become easier to slowly introduce some of the other elements to give your stories more depth and complexity.
- **Start with a familiar audience.** One of the intimidating things about telling stories that sets them apart from everyday conversations is that your audience begins to have greater expectations of you as a speaker. At a minimum they expect to hear a series of complete and somewhat sequential thoughts. From there, the expectations rise to being informed, compelled, entertained, or even emotionally moved. Those expectations can put a lot of pressure on you as a non-native speaker of the language!

This is why it is easier to build your storytelling confidence with familiar faces. You can start by testing out a story with a friend, tutor, or spouse, then asking for feedback on what they thought of your delivery. If you don't have anyone that you can talk to, you can also practice by yourself in front of a mirror, or video record yourself and go back later to critique your performance. Look for areas where you did not use grammar or vocabulary correctly, or portions where you did not clearly express yourself or had awkward pauses. The more you do this, you will see how you improve over time.

- **Try impromptu speaking.** Impromptu (or unplanned) speaking is one of the best ways to practice spontaneity and delivering stories on the fly. After all, most of the time when we tell stories, such as our grocery store example from above, with friends or acquaintances, we rarely think about them ahead of time. Instead, the words just come out after we have a desire to share something with them.

Years ago, I was a member of the Toastmasters International organization. Toastmasters is a worldwide club that allows its members to practice public speaking in a friendly and (most of the time) non-intimidating environment. Most Toastmaster meetings included a section called "Table Topics" during which some members were called upon to give impromptu or unplanned mini-speeches on a random topic. The speeches were typically between 2 to 5 minutes in length, and could include anything that the speaker wanted. They could be funny, insightful, poetic, simply state facts, and could contain literally **anything**. The only thing that really mattered was that the person kept talking during that time.

While learning Spanish, I found a way to incorporate this simple concept in order to improve

my ability to tell stories. I did this by looking up random public speaking topics online, then speaking completely in Spanish between 2 to 5 minutes on that topic while I recorded myself using my laptop camera. After I finished the recording, I would go back and review what I said to evaluate my performance. Even if I had nothing to say, that was beneficial as well, because it allowed me to practice filler words and utterances that would force me to improvise the way I used the language.
Improvisation, as you know, is a necessary skill that all native speakers of a language have.
You can and should take advantage of this exercise. After you do this several times, you will **want** to get in front of someone to get more authentic practice. The ability to tell compelling and interesting stories is something that even native speakers struggle with. Not everyone can do it. Even if you are not great at it, just committing yourself to improving your ability to tell stories shows that you are truly an experienced and knowledgeable speaker of your target language. Don't get discouraged if you feel awkward and strange practicing it initially. Like much of the rest of the advice in this book, with dedicated practice, you **will improve** and eventually will have the ability to enthrall an entire room or online audience with stories about any topic that you can conceive.

- **Take a break.** Am I really suggesting that you **stop** learning a language for a period of time, in a book about learning languages!? Yes I am. While it may seem counterproductive to not study for a while in order to improve, it really can help you.

One reason is simply because your mind needs a rest from particular stimuli once in a while in order to process and accordingly store the information that you've given it.

Have you ever done bench press at the gym with heavy weight, then tried to immediately return the next day to lift the same muscle group again? What happened? It is likely that your muscles were too fatigued for you to even lift the weight.

Your mind works in a similar fashion, even it benefits from a rest day every now and then, so that it can recover, and come back stronger than before.

Taking a break from language learning also allows you to pull back and see all of the progress that you have made, which can provide a much needed confidence to boost you as a student of that language.

Often as language students, we may get caught up on certain aspects of the language that we want to improve on so much, that we forget about the parts of it that we are have already mastered. By taking breaks, we can pull our eyes away from the microscope and see all of the progress that we have made since we began studying the language.

If you have been studying a language consistently for at least 6 months to a year, consider taking a week or two off from deliberate study. It might just be the change that you need that will push you to a higher level of comfort with the language.

General Notes on This Level

You are still a non-native speaker, and that's ok. If one of your goals was to be able to not be seen as a foreigner, then don't be disappointed when I tell you that this is very hard to do. Even if your language is perfectly fluent and your accent is minimal, if native speakers talk to you for long enough, they will probably be able to tell that you are a foreigner. This is the reason that I titled this chapter "native-like" as opposed to "native." No matter how well you speak or can use your target language you will always be viewed as an outsider by some native speakers.

The only people that I know who have been able to pass as native speakers of a language have spent an extensive amount of time living in an area where the language is spoken (think at least 5 or 10 years). Or they married someone who spoke the language and used it as their primary language at home.

Outside of these two extremes, and for the most part uncommon circumstances, you most likely will always be that foreigner with an accent. Which is completely alright. If you are interested in losing your foreign accent, there are services that can help you, but keep in mind that they only tend to be available for more widely spoken languages like English.

Some native speakers won't appreciate your language literacy. Be aware, that just because you are proficient in a certain language does not mean that native speakers will immediately accept you. Although the majority of people will appreciate the fact that you speak their language at such a high level, there will be some who may feel threatened or even get angry that you do. Whether this is because of previous negative experiences with foreigners or a deeply entrenched historical reason, you'll probably never know.

The point is to be aware that if you do not **look** like someone who shares the same ethnic background as someone who could be a native speaker of the language, you will almost always be initially met with at least surprise by native speakers. This surprise is born from the innate human bias that we all share. We expect a person who looks Latino to speak Spanish, and a person who looks like a White American to speak English, so when a different language comes out of a face that doesn't match our expectations, we get surprised.

As a Black American who speaks Japanese, I have experienced this bias too many times to count. For the people who are curious and begin to ask you questions, use it as an opportunity to share some of your culture with them. If you're met with hostility, kindly dismiss yourself and don't let them take away your enthusiasm for the language. Most importantly, don't associate their attitude with that of all native speakers, because most probably don't think that way.

Continue to make mistakes. As you use the language more and more, you will assimilate it so well that it may begin to influence how you speak your native language. This can lead to unconscious mistakes in your speech as you occasionally mix up vowel sounds or sentence structures. Don't worry about it. You probably don't speak your mother tongue perfectly either everyday, so you surely shouldn't expect to do it with a foreign one. Every mistake you make refines your usage of the language a little more over time, even at this high level, so continue to use it as much as possible.

Language atrophy. It is possible that your language skills **will** deteriorate if you don't use them. After I left Japan, my skills ossified so much that I couldn't even hold a basic conversation with it two years after I moved.

The good news is that, if you've reached native-like fluency in the past, you will most likely never completely forget the language. Though you may have to spend some time using it again consistently, it will come back to you should you need it again.

If your skills do worsen, however, return to the appropriate level in this book to reassess yourself and build yourself back up again from there. **The more you studied in the past the easier it will be to bring your language back up to proficient levels.**

Learning and maintaining multiple languages. Now that you've reached a high level in one language, you might consider doing it all over again with another language. Studies show that after you have learned a second language to proficiency, it is much easier to learn a third or even a fourth language.

I can attest that this is true. Becoming highly literate in Spanish made it easier for me to return to Japanese and refine my skills, as well as dabble in a few others including Chinese, Malay, Burmese, and Tamil.

In addition to having the confidence that it is possible for you to learn a foreign language, you will also benefit from having developed a structure for your language learning. You will be able to take advantage of that same structure, to place another language and culture on top of it. This not only makes learning another language easier, but generally makes it more enjoyable, because you won't worry as much about the effectiveness of your learning strategies and can instead focus on the aspects of it that you enjoy.

If you are considering picking up a new language while you continue to study one that you have learned or studied in the past, below are a few suggestions to make life easier for you from someone who has juggled studying three languages at once.

- **Try to study languages from different language families.** This is generally good advice from most advanced polyglots, and it makes a lot of sense. Languages from the same language family, like Spanish and Portuguese for example, tend to have similar vocabulary, grammar, phonology, and syntax, however; the differences between pronunciation, spelling, and small variance in the aforementioned characteristics, can make it very difficult to make significant progress in languages such as these at the same time. It is simply too easy to become confused by all of characteristics of the language.
Languages that are completely unrelated such as Japanese and Spanish, are much better companion languages. They are vastly different from one another and it will be much easier to distinguish them from each other in your mind as you study.
- **Adjust your language goals accordingly.** It should be obvious to note that because you are dividing your time between two languages, you will not make progress in either them as quickly as you would be if

you just studied them one at a time. I say this because, many people (like me) who attempt to study two or more languages at the same time, consider themselves skilled at learning languages and because of this we think that we can make the same amount of progress **at the same time** with all of the languages. I know from personal experience that things don't work that way.

Your own vanity as a self-proclaimed language learning rockstar can impede your ability to effectively learn the languages that you have decided to study. Therefore, if you are going to study two or more languages at a time, then I suggest that you already be at least at an **intermediate** level in one of them. This is because in my opinion, the majority of the heavy lifting when it comes to learning a language is in the beginner and advanced beginner phases when you are learning to make and recognize the sounds of the language. In the intermediate phase, it is easier to settle into a practice routine of rotating between the various activities for improving all modalities of the language.

Trying to learn two or more languages that you have little to no skill in, is usually a bad idea. Typically, you will ultimately find one language more enjoyable than the other and avoid the one that is more difficult for you. In that case, it would be best for you to drop the other language entirely and focus exclusively on the language that is easier for you.

- **Don't do it unless you HAVE TO.** While it might be tempting to study two or more languages at a time, I suggest that you avoid doing it unless you **absolutely have to.** In the end, I think learning two languages at a time is something that makes many of us who love learning languages feel good, but most of us know that it is not a very effective strategy for learning either of those languages to a high level.

Even if you are able to successfully maintain a disciplined study schedule for both or all of the multiple languages for a few weeks or months, your proficiency will probably not exceed the lower intermediate level in any of the languages. This is because as you know by now, the study time required to make significant progress in just one language becomes much larger at that level. Few people can manage to keep up that level of commitment for two or more languages, no matter how skilled or dedicated they are to learning languages.

I can think of very **few** examples outside of a rare national security or military requirement where a person would **have to** learn two or more languages at a time. Even most government or military training that has this requirement, will provide training in the languages **consecutively**, but rarely **simultaneously** with the expectation that you be proficient in both.

If you do decide to seriously learn, study, or practice two or more languages at a time, realize that you are taking on an unnecessary burden, that will most likely produce subpar results in all of the languages involved.

Try Language Chaining. After you have reached the native-like level in one language, why not use that language to learn or practice another? I call this "language chaining." Most people who learn a language begin by using materials that are mostly in their native language, but now that you are at such a high level in another language, using this language to possibly learn a third language is a fantastic idea to further solidify your second language into your memory.

If you can find materials that will allow you to do it, then I highly recommend that you try this. You will see your first target language from a brand new perspective as you see how **it** translates to another language that is not your native language.

A quick warning though, be sure that you are truly at the native-like level before you try this because, if not, it will be very difficult to get much out of the materials that you purchased to learn the third language. For example: if you change the language on your computer to Spanish while attempting to learn Japanese, it will be difficult to learn Japanese if you can barely read Spanish.

Final thoughts on being a native-like speaker. By reaching such a high level of ability in your target language, you should realize and appreciate your achievement. Technically, anyone who has knowledge of a language can claim to be able to "know" it to some degree, but few people can function with their target language as well as they can in their native language. Now you can. Even today with all of the technology that we have at our fingertips, it still remains a rare and exceptional achievement.

If you truly are at this level, and this book has helped you get there in some way, then it has achieved its purpose, and my hope is that you share your new found language literacy with the world in some way. That is the reason why you spent all of this time learning it right?

The language is not just a part of your life at this point, it is a part of you. Barring some catastrophic head injury, it will never leave you, which for a language learning enthusiast is a comforting thought. Your only goal now with this language is to maintain and utilize it as much as possible. How you do that is up to you, but if you're interested, the final portion of this book will provide you some ways to prove to potential clients or other hiring authorities that you mean business with your language.

Native-Like Level Quick Notes

Do (Action Items)

- Learn specialized vocabulary
- Focus on a particular region or dialect
- Watch documentaries, read books and articles online, etc. about the region (in your target language)
- Listen to podcasts about topics that interest you
- Consume entertainment in your target language
- Watch stand-up comedy
- Become a great storyteller
- Start by telling basic stories
- Start with a familiar audience
- Do impromptu speaking to improve
- Take a break for learning the language

Native-Like Level

Do (General Notes)
- Continue to make mistakes
- Use and maintain your skills often to avoid language atrophy
- Only study multiple languages at a time if necessary. If you do study multiple languages follow these guidelines:
- Study languages from different language families
- Adjust your language goals accordingly
- Try language chaining to learn a third language with your second language
- Don't Do It Unless You Have To!

Don't (General Notes)
- Worry about being seen as a non-native speaker
- Pay attention to native speakers who are not appreciative of your language proficiency

The Professional Language Learner's Toolkit (Chapter 7)

From Hobbyist to Professional

Many people learn foreign languages for different reasons. Some do it as a hobby, others just want to be able to connect with people from different cultures around the world. While these and other reasons are good enough to want to become literate in a foreign language, what about those people who want to go a step further and make a liveable wage with their passion for languages? What kinds of credentials, specialized training, or connections should you have to turn your passion into profit?

Unlike most language learners, my goal was always to use my language skills to put food on the table. If you can identify with that, or you have ever thought of seriously using your skills in the labor market, this next section will give you some factors to consider before you make your next move.

Types of Language Jobs

Jobs related to languages generally fall into 3 different categories. Don't believe every job description that you read. While language skills may be a **preference** for some jobs, they may be a hard **requirement** for others. Additionally, with the availability of internet resources it has become increasingly easier to **combine** languages with other established careers or hobbies. Let's look at examples of all three.

Language Preferred Jobs. These are jobs that **prefer** that you have language skills for occasional use, but for the most part do not require the language. It could be that the job is situated in place that serves a community where numerous speakers of a certain language live, or has many clients that speak another language. Either way there may be some days when you use your language heavily, and not at all on others. Job advertisements may also require you to speak **some** or **have a good understanding** of the language. Some of these jobs include:

- Certain retail jobs
- Certain sales jobs
- Flight attendants (depends on airline)
- Hotel Management jobs
- Many service jobs

Language Required Jobs. In some jobs it is absolutely mandatory that you are fluent in and/or possess a high level of literacy or proficiency in the language that is demanded for the position. You may be required to interact with native speakers of the language, or analyze, translate, or transcribe materials from the target language to your native language or vice-versa.

Examples of these jobs include:

- Interpreter
- Translator
- Language Teacher
- Subtitler/Localizer
- Language Analyst
- Foreign Correspondent (Journalism)

Although wages in these jobs tend to be the highest that a language professional can command, many of these jobs are freelance or contract positions. This means that work may not always be guaranteed, and few offer any of the benefits like healthcare, retirement plans, or sick days. This is something to take into consideration depending on your life circumstances.

Language "hybrid" jobs. Most of the jobs that I've mentioned up to this point are traditional language jobs. They are the positions that most people think of when it comes to jobs that allow them to use a foreign language. But are there any other options? One of the benefits of the internet age that we live in, is that languages can be combined with almost any other discipline to form a job that can provide you with income. Here are some examples of jobs that are non-traditional but focus on language use.

- Language coaching (online or in person) (language + teaching/coaching)
- Bilingual Podcaster (language + broadcasting/journalism)

- Lawyer (specializing in foreign clients) (language + law)

There are countless other examples out there. The point is that you may have to think outside of the box and find a creative way to make a living with your languages. While traditional jobs may offer in general more stability, a non-traditional job may allow you to customize how you use your language, and ultimately allow you to make as much money as you want with it.

The key is to think about the things that you like to do and are knowledgeable in and how you can integrate foreign languages into that equation. If you like bugs, perhaps you could start a podcast focused on bugs only found in South and Latin America, for Spanish speakers and English speakers. This is just one example, but it shows what's possible when you combine languages with another passion.

Language Credentialing

Language credentialing can be a controversial topic among language learners. On the one hand, I know that being able to pass a written or oral test in a language does not always mean that you are proficient with the language. However, I also know that institutions, businesses, and clients that hire language professionals need (and enjoy) some kind of standard to evaluate how well someone can comprehend and use the language.

I wanted to include this section because I feel like many people who love and study languages, do not take the extra step to earn any type of credentials in their languages. Whether it is because they know, in reality, that their actual skill in the language isn't as proficient as they claim it to be, or because they can already function well enough in the language for their needs, I have no idea. But the fact is that if you want your language skills to be taken seriously by any hiring entity or potential business partners, you **should** consider earning some type of credential that proves that you are proficient with the language. Luckily, with the power of technology, you no longer have to register for a college level course to display your language skills. (We all know those classes don't always ensure that you know the language anyway.) There are multiple ways to set yourself apart from the competition that are just as effective and easier to access.

Standing Out As a Language Professional

Now that you are aware of what types of jobs are available for you as a language enthusiast, it's time to talk about ways that you can convince clients or hiring authorities to hire you. We'll discuss some of the pros and cons of each option, and ultimately determine how effective they are at making you stand out from the crowd.

Language Degrees

For those of you who, like me, already have a degree in a foreign language, you most likely know how much it is worth in the working world. If you are currently working towards a degree in a language, I'm sad to be the one to tell you that that piece of paper isn't worth much to potential employers, when it comes to proving your actual skill with that particular language. Like a 4-year degree in any other subject, the language degree shows people that you had the discipline and knowledge to earn the degree, but not necessarily that you could perform any tasks attached to it. This is especially true for a language degree.

The point is that, even if you have a Master's degree in Spanish doesn't mean that you are fluent in Spanish. This is especially true if a long time has passed since you obtained the degree. The only positions that I know of that require a graduate level degree in a language tend to be teaching positions at traditional 4-year universities. Not only are these positions very few in number, but just as in most teaching positions, you will probably not be using the language with your students at a high level as much as you think, since most of them probably won't be able to speak fluently.

BOTTOM LINE. A language degree from a 4-year institution probably won't help you get a language job. It definitely does not prove that you are proficient with the language either.

Online Language Courses

With the availability of language courses online, it has never been easier to learn or brush up on a foreign language. Some of the advantages of these courses include

- Generally low cost (at least compared to most traditional brick and mortar schools)
- Usually available 24/7

- Often you can receive one-on-one feedback if you are willing to pay for it
- Easy to fit into your schedule

I have taken several courses online, and each one helped me improve my Spanish in some way. If you complete one of these courses, try to get some type of proof of completion that you can show to potential employers or clients. They may not ask for it if your skills are good enough, but it's always good to have it just in case.

BOTTOM LINE. Online language courses are an excellent and affordable way to boost your language skills. The course certification is also a strong indicator that you can actually speak and understand the language.

Formal Tests

It should come as no surprise that taking and passing a formal test in your language (if one exists) will always help you stand out to employers or clients. Many of the tests are internationally recognized and can even help you find work overseas in a country where your language is spoken. (See Appendix 2 for a list of official language tests).

Of course, many of these tests are quite challenging, and may require months of dedicated study time to pass. Additionally, the tests are often expensive and may require you to travel to take them, since they are often only administered in larger cities. But, in the end they may be the gateway to much greater opportunities with your chosen language.

BOTTOM LINE. Passing a formal test will definitely help your resume stand out among others as a language professional.

Formal Language Immersion Programs

Language immersions can be incredible experiences. After my 4-week language immersion in Japan as a college student, not only had my Japanese improved quite a bit, but I had made valuable connections in the country with Japanese citizens and of course, with other people who were also participating in the program. Additionally, I had the opportunity to explore the Western side of Japan in a way that most tourists will never get to experience. I'll never forget my time over there, and if you are ever fortunate enough to participate in one of these programs you will likely reap as much benefit from it as I did.

The best thing about these types of immersion programs is that most of them, in general, are very well-planned. You won't have to worry about where you will stay, what primary activities to do during the day (or at night sometimes either), and they may even pay for smaller things like public transportation or certain meals. Better still, is the fact that you will most likely be traveling in a group, with arranged contacts in the country that you are traveling to. All of this makes the experience that much more enjoyable, since you won't have to worry about being alone in a strange country. All of the above allows you to focus on getting the most out of your trip. Whether your goal is to improve your language, absorb as much of the culture and cuisine as possible, or just to take a long overdue sabbatical from your ordinary existence, the trip has you covered.

Unfortunately, for all of the previously mentioned positives of these programs, there are also annoyances that can be equally frustrating. For one, the majority of the programs that exist are run by schools and governments. This means that if you are not an undergrad or a graduate student, or a potential government employee that might benefit from some type of immersion trip, you probably will not qualify for these types of immersions. You will most likely have to do it through a private company or on your own, which will be discussed in detail shortly.

If you are a high school or college student, then you are in the best position to take advantage of a formal immersion program. Your school could pay for some of it, and you might even get some kind of stipend while you're abroad. However, these programs tend to be fairly competitive, due to the cost that it takes to coordinate flights, transportation, lodging, meals, and whatever other excursions might be included. So be sure to do everything that you can to meet the prerequisites established by your schools programs.

As I mentioned earlier, non-college attending adults have no choice but to go through a private company for an immersion trip. They often provide similar experiences as those offered by governments and schools, but you will most likely have to pay more out of pocket for it. Although I have never done an immersion with a private company, many of the ones that I have researched for this book are fairly expensive, and of course require you to be available for several weeks or even months consecutively to be able to participate. Before you apply and potentially spend thousands of dollars, ask yourself what you really want to get out of the experience, because there might be a cheaper way to do it that doesn't require as much time or money.

If you decide that you can't afford the cost of the program and don't have the time to uproot yourself and live overseas for an extended period of time, you can always make plans to travel on your own.

In the end, any time that you can tell a potential client or employer that you spent time in a place or country as part of a formal immersion program it will go a long way toward establishing your credibility with them. Even if all you did was drink, party, and travel while you were there.

BOTTOM LINE. Formal immersion programs provide tremendous "street credit" to your language skills. Additionally, they can be a very valuable experiences for your language skills, language career, and personal development. But they can be costly, somewhat selective, and require a large time commitment.

Informal Language Immersion

What I consider "informal immersion" others might simply call taking a brief trip or vacation to a place that predominantly speaks your target language. You probably won't be able to stay with a host family (although you could use AirBnB or any other service that allows you to crash at a foreigner's house overseas), but you will have a lot more flexibility with what you do and see in the country, than with a formal immersion program.

Traveling on your own or with someone else can actually be cheaper than paying for a formal immersion program, because you can omit certain meals, excursions, or extras that are considered mandatory in those trips.

The only drawback to a personalized informal immersion, is that it can be difficult to sell as a resume builder unless you actually conducted some kind of official business there. This could include holding a meeting with clients in the country, conducting onsite research for a potential project, or almost any other purpose, as long as you can tie it to your work somehow. You will have to get creative with how you pass off the immersion as professional experience, so it doesn't come off as a vacation. At the end of the day, much like formal immersion programs, traveling to a country or location where your language is spoken and **using** it there, will always give you unofficial street credit with native speakers, employers, and clients especially if your target language is not widely spoken anywhere else.

BOTTOMLINE. If done correctly, an informal immersion can be a cheaper alternative to a formal trip, and can be just as valuable and transformative. It may, however, take some creativity to make employers and clients see it that way.

Non-Class Language Resources as Experience

I use the term "non-class language resources" to classify any language tool that does not fit neatly into the category of an online course or a well-known language program like Rosetta Stone or Duolingo, but still serves the purpose of teaching the language. If the definition seems too broad, that's because it's meant to be. There are thousands of language resources that would fit into this miscellaneous category, and that number is increasing quickly everyday as new apps and programs are developed.

Another reason I included this section is that, now, anyone who is in the beginner, or in the "language interested phase", is more likely to download one of these apps or visit a free resource online, before committing financially to a paid course on or offline to study the language. This just makes sense, with the vast amount of free language resources that are available. Remember earlier in the book when I mentioned that the beginner level market for language tools was so crowded that, ironically, even the language interested are quickly turned off because they don't know where to begin? Many of those resources would most likely fall into this category. This is especially true for commonly studied languages like Spanish, French, or Chinese, for which there are many options to learn the basics of the language. I predict that this trend will only grow in the future, as more people in the developing world get access to the internet and realize that establishing a small online course for their rare or exotic language could net them a potential huge profit, but that's a discussion for another time, or another book.

An example of one of these tools is the Japanese Dictionary app. Though, true to its name, it is indeed a Japanese dictionary with over 175,000 entries and over 50,000 example sentences with text-to-speech functionality, it also has a robust Kanji dictionary that allows for writing practice, spaced repetition flashcards, and many other features. It's basically an all-in-one Japanese classroom that puts my old Japanese textbooks to shame. Any person interested in studying Japanese could very easily use this powerful app on its own to achieve a high level of literacy in the language. This is just one example of a non-classroom language resource for one language. There are hundreds of other similar apps and even websites that provide a similar level of content in other languages, and can be just as effective.

Right now using these non-classroom language resources to learn foreign languages is very common, but can they help you stand out as a language professional? The answer is it depends.

We all know that not all language apps are created equal and they surely are not all created with the same training philosophy. While 100 hours on Duolingo might mean that you reached a high beginner or even lower intermediate level as a speaker, that same 100 hours spent with a program like Glossika, could mean that your level may be upper intermediate or even low advanced. And this is only in the speaking and listening modalities. One follows a more traditional language teaching model, while the other is a bit more abstract and highly repetition based.

This is just comparing two of the thousands of online apps and programs that exist to teach people languages. The general problem with any resources that fall into this category for people interested in your resumé is that the disparity between the quality of the app's content, how much you used it, and how well you can speak, understand, or use the language is often too great for them to quantify. Additionally, with how quickly new language tools rise and fall in the online market, they may not even know what you are talking about when you mention a certain tool. It's simply too hard to keep up with them all, especially if they're not looking to learn a language themselves. (Big surprise, most people are not.)

For that reason, I would say that for the most part these apps and programs should remain off of your resumé. An exception to this that comes to mind is if the company you are applying for has adopted a certain language platform for training or general use, then of course it would be valuable to include it on there. For example, I know that my former middle school used Duolingo to teach students the basics of Spanish, so some knowledge of that app would definitely be beneficial if I ever applied for a job there.

I imagine that in the future, the trends above will change and it will be more valuable to include certain apps and programs on a resumé. As new technology is developed and a way to standardize the quality of these apps comes into existence people's perspective of the efficacy of many non-class language resources may change. Until that day comes, use the apps and programs to maintain or improve your skills, but look to one of the previous methods as a way to tell employers and clients that you are knowledgeable with the language.

BOTTOM LINE. Non-class language resources are great tools to practice your language, but you should not rely on them to help you standout as a language professional.

The Future of Foreign Languages (Chapter 8)

This book came about because of my love of foreign languages and cultures. It's a passion that I know many of you share with me and that I hope to continue to be able to maintain in some way for the rest of my life. However, no matter how much passion and zeal we have for learning languages, these still cannot overcome the march of technology and its impact on the future of languages.

As our world becomes increasingly more connected and technological advances continue at their blinding pace, what will happen to our need to become literate in a foreign language? Will we even need to learn one? Every day, new apps capable of competent written and voice translations are being developed, chatbots are becoming increasingly more sophisticated at mimicking human interaction, and other technological advances are leaping forward in body modification with technology. These are just a few of the advances that are happening right now, that have the potential to significantly impact not just how we learn languages, but how we communicate with each other and the algorithm driven machines that we will inevitably create in the future.

What does all this have to do with learning a foreign language? In my mind, technology will impact world languages in two keys areas: acquisition and language necessity.

Acquisition. The ways in which we learn languages has changed dramatically in just the last two decades. Before the internet, in order to learn the writing system for a language like Japanese, you needed to get your hands on the handful of materials available for Westerners and have a lot of patience to painstakingly look up and practice writing individual kanji characters in order commit them to memory. That was just for learning the writing system!

Now, many resources have spaced repetition systems (SRS) loaded with thousands of kanji characters, words, example sentences, AND memory mnemonics. These programs have made it much easier to access and learn the language. This same thing is happening with many other languages around the world, including less commonly spoken ones.

With current technology, it has never been easier in all of human history to learn a foreign language. I predict, in the coming years with more sophisticated tech like chatbots, augmented reality, and artificial intelligence, it will become even easier. Imagine being able to speak with a native sounding Chinese program who will not only have a conversation with you, but also provide you with instant feedback based on parameters like grammar and pronunciation that **YOU** want to improve on, all from the comfort of your living room via augmented or virtual reality. I assure you that this tech is already well in-development and it will become mainstream sooner than you or I can anticipate. Maybe it will even have already supplanted traditional learning methods by the time you read this book.

Language Necessity. With all of these technological advances, will we even need to learn a foreign language in the future? Would you want to? The ability to encode, decode, and translate spoken speech already exists, but let's just say that some of the results have been less than impressive. Programs often mistake certain expressions (especially idioms) for more literal translations with hilarious results, and the output often does not sound like a desirable conversation partner. This field is still in its adolescence, but in as little as 5 years, someone is going to figure out how to do it right and make it available for all of us. After this revolutionary device that more or less can mimic a human speaking English or Spanish comes into our homes, lives, and businesses, what will become of our need to learn foreign languages?

Honestly I don't have the answer to this question. While I feel like most people would always prefer to speak any language with a fellow human being, I think about myself back in 2003.

I remember shortly after getting my first cellphone, a Nokia flip phone, that everyone was starting this new thing called "texting." I can remember telling one of my friends, "Why the hell would I type a message with what I have to say rather than just pressing call and having an actual conversation?" You all know what has happened since then. If you're like me, texting is now your primary means of communication, with phone calls reserved for work or extended conversations with family members and close friends. If history is any indication, technology may cause an upheaval in many markets, and that includes language learning and language fields.

The future can be very scary, because none of us knows exactly what will happen. While I can't say if this entire book will be obsolete and unnecessary in ten years, I can tell you what I'm doing to prepare for the inevitable arrival of technology's impact on language learning and the language industry. These are things that you can start to do today as well, even if you feel like it already may be too late.

- **Education.** Educate yourself on trends related to the language industry. Pay attention to new technology by following influencers on social media, reading tech magazines, and doing general internet research. In this case knowledge is power, and it may help you understand how to make certain technology better fit into your overall approach to language learning.
- **Look for hybrid opportunities.** Foreign language skills are still very valuable right now. It is a great time to merge your passion for language learning with another skill or passion that you have. As I mentioned in the hybrid jobs section, there are an infinite number of ways to combine languages with other skills. I just takes a little outside-of-the-box thinking, and patience to experiment with what will work for you.
- **Do your thing.** Just because certain languages are more widely spoken than others and technology will certainly impact them first (think Spanish over Bulgarian), doesn't mean that you should (or

shouldn't) learn languages that are less popular. If you really like Iceland, and you want to live there because your partner is from Iceland, by all means study Icelandic. You will probably learn it faster because you have a greater incentive to learn it. Don't let technology or any other trends (including negative media perception) influence what language you study. Do your thing and find a way to fit it into your life.

New Hope

I understand that the previous section may have you questioning whether it is worth the time to even learn a language at all. If you're a little afraid now, consider it a wake-up call to the reality of the world that we live in. However, the word "future" is the header of the section for a reason. As for the present, the world needs more passionate, talented, and empathetic language learners now more than ever.

With the global community merging closer together every day through social media and increased cultural interaction, people need intermediaries among those communities to help them better communicate with and understand each other. That's where you come in. And no, you don't need to be able to speak like a native speaker to have an impact. Even basic skills, a desire to improve in the language, and a good attitude are useful for helping you make an impact.

Strengthening Communities

The community level is where newer language learners can have the greatest impact right now.

While the need for language professionals overseas and in high profile positions, may remain for the near future, demand for literate language professionals continues to rise at the community level. This is especially true in the United States, which is home to one of the most culturally diverse populations on the planet.

There are more opportunities at the community level to bridge language and culture gaps and to use your language abilities to help facilitate understanding among others. Please don't be old-fashioned and limit the word "community" to the physical neighborhood in which you reside. There are thousands of communities online on Facebook, YouTube, Reddit, and other social media platforms that have members from all around the world, who could use your help. The perspective of one person who can speak the language and can empathize with the cultural and historical points of view of others could change the other person's entire view of the community as a whole. In this way, you become not only a student of the language, but also an ambassador of your country, ethnicity, and culture. Yes, even you can have that much impact.

Maybe you won't make much or any money doing this, but you will have played a role in making that community a little safer and more welcoming for others who don't share your background.

Conclusion

I wrote this book because I wanted to give other people who share my passion for foreign languages a practical guide to learning one on their own. I know how difficult and frustrating it can be to spend months or years studying a language, and still not be able to speak or understand it. I also know how tedious it can be to wade through the virtually endless sea of materials and information available out there to find what you personally need to be able to learn it. Let this book serve as your beacon and guide to helping you meet your language goals. If you desire to become a language professional like me, then keep in mind the things that I discussed in the final section of the book as you work to establish your career. Know that you provide a valuable skill to any business or client that you work with, no matter the circumstance.

For as long as I can remember, I've seen being able to speak a foreign language as a kind of magic power, akin to being able to fly. Instead of being able to soar over the city skyline like Superman, a person that could speak a foreign language could connect people by making the sounds that one person utters understable to another. And I still think it's incredible.

The fact that such a complex cognitive task could be done by any person always fascinated me. After I learned that I could learn that skill and possess that magic myself, I began to fight harder through the initial embarrassment and shame that we all inevitably meet when we begin mumbling and babbling in a language that we have never known. I was also further incentivized by the look in someone's eyes when they feel understood in a language that is their own. It is a sign to me that my magic, as imperfect as it may be sometimes, is working and growing. That's how I always want it to be for me, and I want that for you too. It's not about flawless grammar, perfect pronunciation, or having a native speaker accent; it's about connecting with people on a level that we all desire from others. That is true magic,

Tower of Babbling

and you have the potential within you to make it as well. Now go make some magic.

Appendix 1, Resources

Initially, I was hesitant to include a list of actual resources that I personally used to become fluent in Spanish and improve myself in other languages. Technology moves so quickly that many lists run the risk of becoming outdated before the book is published.

Still, I figured that it would be helpful to include one for those of you who are interested in learning a language, but have no idea where to start.

The list isn't just the name of the app, program, or book. I've also included what modality (reading, speaking, writing, listening) it can help you with for further guidance.

- Glossika - Use for: Speaking, Listening
- LingQ - Use for: Reading, Listening, Vocabulary
- Linguee.com - Use for: Vocabulary, Reading
- Forvo.com - Use for: Speaking, Pronunciation
- DeepL (Translator) - Use for: Translation, Reading
- italki.com - Use for: Speaking, Writing, Listening
- Anki Flashcards - Use for: Vocabulary
- Duolingo - Use for: Speaking, Grammar, Listening
- wordreference.com - Use for: Vocabulary, Translation
- Clozemaster - Use for: Vocabulary
- MeetUp.com - Use to find speaking groups
- YouTube.com - Use to find any type of tools
- italki.com - Use to find tutors and receive feedback for writing
- Medium.com - Use for writing practice
- Netflix.com - Use to watch TV series/comedy in your target language

Appendix 2, Formal Tests

Here is a list of formal tests for certification in various languages. Some must be taken in the country where the language is spoken, but might be worth the trip if you want to stand out as a language professional with that language.

American Council on the Teaching of Foreign Languages (ACFTL) Oral Proficiency Interview (OPI) Tests

The test consists of a 15 - 30 minute telephonic conversation between the candidate and a certified ACFTL tester. There is also a computerized version of the test that is done with pre-recorded questions called the OPIc, for certain languages.

The OPI is a certified test that serves as proof of spoken proficiency in any of the following languages:

Afrikaans	Burmese	French
Akan-Twi	Cambodian	Ga
Albanian	Cantonese	Georgian
Algerian	Cebuano	German
Amharic	Chavacano	Greek
Arabic	Czech	Gujarati
Armenian	Danish	Haitian Creole
Azerbaijani	Dari	Hausa
Baluchi	Dutch	Hebrew
Bamana	Egyptian	Hindi
Bengali	English	Hmong
Bosnian	Ewe	Hungarian
Bulgarian	Finnish	Igbo

Tower of Babbling

Ilocano	Mandingo-Bambara	Syrian
Indonesian		Tagalog
Iraqi	Marathi	Taiwanese
Italian	Marshallese	Tajik
Japanese	Mongolian	Tamil
Javanese	Nepali	Tausug
Jordanian	Norwegian	Telugu
Kashmiri	Palestinian	Thai
Kazakh	Pashto	Tigrinya
Kikongo	Persian Farsi	Tunisian
Kinyarwanda	Polish	Turkish
Kirundi	Portuguese	Turkmen
Korean	Punjabi	Uighur
Krio	Romanian	Ukrainian
Kurdish	Russian	Urdu
Lao	Serbian/Croatian	Uzbek
Latin	Sindhi	Vietnamese
Levantine	Sinhalese	Wolof
Libyan	Slovak	Wu
Lingala	Somali	Yemeni
Luganda	Spanish	Yoruba
Malay	Sudanese	Zulu
Malayalam	Swahili	
Mandarin	Swedish	

https://www.languagetesting.com/language-selection?language=certif&submitUri=https%3A%2F%2Fwww.languagetesting.com%2Fcertifications-tests%2Fcertifications

Appendix 2 – Foreign Language Tests

American Sign Language

American Sign Language Proficiency Interview

https://www.ets.org/praxis/ct/aslpi/

Arabic

Arabic Language Proficiency Test
https://www.arabacademy.com/features/arabic-language-proficiency-test/

Bahasa Indonesian

Uji Kemajiran Berbahasa Indonesia (UKBI) also known as Test of Indonesian as a Foreign Language (TOIFL)
http://www.lia.com.sg/site/

Bahasa Melayu

The Malay Language Proficiency Certification Test for Non-Malaysians
http://alamiyyah.usim.edu.my/en/current-students/skbmw

European Consortium for the Certificate of Attainment in Modern Languages (ECL)

They offer language testing for languages spoken in some European Union member countries. Languages available include

- English
- Polish
- Hungarian

- German
- French
- Italian
- Slovakian
- Spanish
- Russian
- Bulgarian
- Romanian
- Serbian
- Czech
- Croatian
- Hebrew

Burmese

Myanmar Language Test
http://www.mlt-myanmar.com/

Chinese - Mandarin

Hanyu Shuiping Kaoshi (HSK) - Covers reading, writing, and listening/comprehension

HSK Speaking Test - For speaking only
https://www.chinaeducenter.com/en/exams.php

Test of Chinese as a Foreign Language (TOCFL) - For learners of Mandarin in Taiwan
https://www.sc-top.org.tw/english/RD/test1.php

Spoken Chinese Test - A 20 minute test that measures speaking ability

Appendix 2 – Foreign Language Tests

https://www.pearsonassessments.com/products/100000772/spoken-chinese-test-sct.html#tab-details

Business Chinese Test (BCT)
http://english.hanban.org/node_8000.htm

Czech

Czech Language Certificate Exam
http://ujop.cuni.cz/en/exam/czech-language-certificate-exam

Danish

CLAVIS Danish Proficiency Test
https://www.clavis.org/eng/for-students/danish-language-proficiency-test

Dutch

Nederlands als Tweede Taal - NT2 (Dutch as a Second Language Test)
https://www.staatsexamensnt2.nl/item/state-exams-dutch-as-a-second

CNaVT or Certificaat Nederlands als Vreemde Taal (Certificate of Dutch as Foreign Language)
http://cnavt.org/

English

Babbel English Test powered by Cambridge English

CAL BEST Literacy

CAL BEST Plus 2.0

The Canadian Academic English Language Assessment (CAEL)
https://www.cael.ca/

Duolingo English Test
https://englishtest.duolingo.com/

E3PT - English3 Proficiency Test
http://english3.com/english3-profiency-test.php

E3J1 - English Interview (Speaking Test)
http://english3.com/j1-interview.php

EF Standard English Test
https://www.efset.org/

English Language Skills Assessment
http://www.icls.edu/english-language-programs/english-skills-assessment/

IELPT - International English Language Proficiency Test
https://www.ielts.org/en-us/

iTEP - International Test of English Proficiency
https://www.itepexam.com/

Language Cert
http://www.languagecert.org/en/Pages/LanguageCert-Home.aspx

Malaysian University English Test (MUET)
https://eduadvisor.my/muet/

STEP - EIKEN - Test in Practical English Proficiency (Japan)
http://www.eiken.or.jp/eiken/en/eiken-tests/

TOEFL - Test of English as a Foreign Language

Appendix 2 – Foreign Language Tests

https://www.ets.org/toefl

TOEIC - Test of English for International Communication
https://www.ets.org/toeic

TrackTest English Proficiency
https://tracktest.eu/

Estonian

Estonian Language Proficiency Exam
https://www.innove.ee/en/examinations-and-tests/estonian-language-proficiency-examinations/

Finnish

Finnish National Language Certificate (Required for Finnish citizenship)
https://www.oph.fi/english/services/yki

French

TEF - Test d'évaluation du français (French Assessment Test)

https://www.lefrancaisdesaffaires.fr/tests-diplomes/test-evaluation-francais-tef/

TCF - Test de connaissance du français
http://www.ciep.fr/es/tcf

Galician

CELGA - Certificado en lingua galega
http://www.lingua.gal/o-galego/aprendelo/celga

German

Deutsches Sprachdiplom Stufe I and II
https://www.kmk.org/themen/deutsches-sprachdiplom-dsd.html

TestDaF - Test Deutsch als Fremdsprache
https://www.testdaf.de/

Greek

Greek Language Certification
http://www.greek-language.gr/certification/

Irish

Teastas Eorpach na gaeilge (Irish Language Proficiency Test)
http://www.teg.ie/english.167.html

Italian

Certificazione di Italiano come Lingua Straniera (Certificate of Italian as a Foreign Language)
https://www.sas.upenn.edu/italians/resources/cils

Certificato di Conoscenza della Lingua Italiana
https://www.europassitalian.com/learn/certification-cils/

Japanese

JLPT - Japanese Language Proficiency Test
https://www.jlpt.jp/e/

BJT - Business Japanese Proficiency Test
http://www.kanken.or.jp/bjt/english/

Appendix 2 — Foreign Language Tests

Kazakh

KAZTEST
http://www.testcenter.kz/en/about/sistema-otsenki-urovnya-vladeniya-kazakhskim-yazykom-kaztest/

Klingon

Klingon Language Certificate
https://www.kli.org/activities/klcp/

Korean

Korean Proficiency Exam
http://exam.ybmnet.co.kr/kpe/eng_main.asp

TOPIK - Test of Proficiency in Korean
https://www.topikguide.com/topik-overview/

Latvian

State Language Proficiency Certificate in Latvian
https://visc.gov.lv/en/stlang/

Lithuanian

Level Examinations of Language Proficiency for Lithuanian
http://www.lsk.flf.vu.lt/en/department/testing/level-examinations/general-information/

Norwegian

Norsk Språktest - Folkeuniversitetet (Test of Norwegian Language) https://www.folkeuniversitetet.no/Artikler/Spraaktester/Test-i-norsk-hoeyere-nivaa

Polish

Certificate Examinations in Polish as a Foreign Language
https://www.lazarski.pl/en/offer/foreign-language-courses/polish-as-a-foreign-language/state-certificate-examinations-in-polish-as-a-foreign-language/

Portuguese (Brazilian)

CELPE-Bras - Brazilian Certificate of Proficiency in Portuguese for Foreigners
http://www.portuguesdobrasil.com.br/certificate-proficiency-brazilian-portuguese-celpe-bras-exam/

Portuguese (European)

CAPLE - Centro de Avaliação de Português Língua Estrangeira (Centre for Evaluation of the Portuguese Language)
http://caple.letras.ulisboa.pt/

Russian

Test of Russian as a Foreign Language
http://russian-test.com/eng/tests/torfl/

Serbo-Croatian

Serbo-Croatian Language Test
http://www.srpskijezik.edu.rs/index.php?id=1160&jzk=sh

Slovak

Slovak Language Certificate Exam
https://cdv.uniba.sk/en/ilps/slovak-language-certificate-exam/

Spanish

SIELE - Servicio Internacional de Evaluación de la Lengua Española
https://siele.org/

CELA - Certificado de Español como Lengua Adicional
http://www.cepe.unam.mx/cela/

Swedish

Swedex
http://www.folkuniversitetet.se/In-English/Swedex_In_English/

Stockholm Chamber of Commerce Certificate in Business Swedish
https://studyinsweden.se/plan-your-studies/learn-swedish/proficiency-tests/

Thai

The Chulalongkorn University Proficiency Test of Thai as a Foreign Language
http://www.sti.chula.ac.th/academic/non-native/CU-TFL

Turkish

Turkish Proficiency Exam

https://www.yee.org.tr/en/content/turkish-proficiency-exam-tys

Vietnamese

VINATEST - Kì thi đánh giá năng lực Tiếng Việt
https://www.vnu.edu.vn/ttsk/?C2091/N16418/Bo-tieu-chuan-va-de-thi-danh-gia-nang-luc-tieng-Viet-cho-hoc-vien-nuoc-ngoai:-danh-gia-toan-dien-va-khach-quan-hon.htm

Welsh

WJEC - Welsh Joint Education Committee Test
http://www.wjec.co.uk/appointees/

www.ingramcontent.com/pod-product-compliance
Lightning Source LLC
Chambersburg PA
CBHW071232080526
44587CB00013BA/1586